Lotus Path: Praticing the Lotus Sutra
Volume 1

Lotus Path: Praticing the Lotus Sutra
Volume 1

By Ryusho Jeffus

Copyright 2014

Myosho-ji, Wonderful Voice Buddhist Temple
2208 Eastway Dr.
Charlotte, NC 28205

License Notes

All rights reserved under International and Pan-American Copyright Conventions. This book, or parts thereof, may not be reproduced in any form without written permission except by a reviewer who may quote brief passages in a review. All photographs, including cover are by Ryusho Jeffus and may not be reproduced without written permission.

ISBN-13: 978-1494986322
ISBN-10: 1494986329

Quotations from the Lotus Sutra:
The Lotus Sutra
The Sutra of the Lotus Flower of the Wonderful Dharma
Translated from Kumarajiva's version of
The Saddharmapundarika-Sutra
Third Edition
by Senchu Murano
Copyright 2012 Nichiren Shu

Dear Reader:

Thank you for purchasing this book of essays, which I hope will help you deepen your faith in and practice of Buddhism. I also hope this book may be a catalyst in helping you make changes in your life so you can become happy in the Dharma of the Lotus Sutra and enlightened.

The practice of Buddhism is about changing our lives deep at the core. Buddhism calls on us to examine the causes of our suffering in brutal honesty. After making this self-assessment we then take the next step and make the necessary changes so we can free ourselves from the cycle of suffering in ignorance.

The essays in the book are short; usually only several hundred words. It is possible to read them quite quickly. That however, is not what I intended and so I have concluded each essay with either some questions for you to consider or suggestions for actions you might decide would be beneficial.

You will get the most value out of this book if you take your time and use the essays and the follow-up comments as tools. Use the book sparingly, sampling each essay as if it were a most delicious candy. This book will be of the most value to you if you actually try to use it as a tool for making changes in your life.

Please take your time and enjoy these essays. I hope they encourage you to deepen your faith and practice of the Lotus Sutra.

With Gassho

Ryusho, Shonin

Hidden Treasure

Buried in a farm field near Frome in Somerset, Britain, the largest collection of ancient Roman coins was discovered by an amateur treasure hunter, Dave Crisp. This collection consisted of 52,000 bronze and silver coins dating from the 3rd century CE. Among the collection were coins minted by self-proclaimed emperor Carausius. The estimated value of the treasure, weighing roughly 350 pounds, was around $5 million.

When I first heard of this I immediately thought about this passage from the Lotus Sutra. "We have obtained unsurpassed treasures although we did not seek them." - Lotus Sutra, Chapter IV.

We may each wish that we could find such a buried treasure as Mr. Crisp found, however in Buddhism we are directed not to seek the treasures of the storehouse or material wealth, but to focus on treasures of the heart. Through the teachings of the Lotus Sutra we are able to uncover the hidden treasure of Buddhahood that is buried deep within our lives.

When Mr. Crisp first uncovered his treasure he first dug up a small bronze coin. If Crisp had stopped with that first coin, thinking that there was nothing more; the remainder of the 350 pounds of coins would have gone uncovered. It is similar for us as we practice Buddhism. Being satisfied with small gains thinking that we have achieved what we have not can cause us to miss the greater treasure of Enlightenment.

Approaching Buddhism as a practice of 'self-improvement' only, that is as a way to do self-help, is like being satisfied by the small bronze coin. While it is true that we do gain self-improvement by our practice, it is the greater goal of complete liberation from suffering and the attainment of Enlightenment that is the spiritual goal of our Buddhist practice.

> If you were to list your goals, would most of them be material or would spiritual goals be the majority?
>
> How much do you expect material things will bring you happiness?
>
> What is your happiness conditioned upon?

Safety Chain

In the Lotus Sutra, Chapter XI, a great stupa appears before the gathered assembly listening to Shakyamuni preach the Lotus Sutra. Inside this stupa resides Many Treasures Buddha who has vowed to be present whenever and wherever the Lotus Sutra is being taught. The folks who were assembled wanted to look at Many Treasures Buddha and asked Shakyamuni if they could see inside. At this point the Buddha called back all of his emanations who had been teaching throughout the universe, he purified the world, and then proceeded to open the door to the stupa.

When we begin to practice and study Buddhism, we begin to open the door to our lives; we open our door, our inner door.

But whom do we open the door to? It could be said that we open the door to no one but ourselves.

It is similar to the opening of the door to the great stupa of Many Treasures, the opening of the door to the practice of Buddhism. We practice the Lotus Sutra so that we can purify our lands, so that we can be of one mind and one body focused on living in the present both fully and mindfully. We open our door to reveal the Many Treasures Buddha that resides within ourselves and we also invite the Eternal Buddha to manifest in our lives.

Frequently doors in our homes have safety chains installed, which allows us to partially open the door and keeps out intruders. In our Buddhist practice we need to remove our safety chain and fully open the door. It is important to daily make efforts to gradually open the door of our life fully and completely to the Buddha that resides within us.

The Buddha Many Treasures invited Shakyamuni to sit beside him in the stupa once the door was opened. There was no safety chain on that stupa; otherwise the Buddha could not have entered. So too in our practice of Buddhism we must remove the safety chain from our life's door and fully embrace our practice so that we can realize the complete benefit of the Lotus Sutra in our lives.

> Can you name some ways in which you limit yourself and your practice of Buddhism?
>
> What comes first in your life? Daily activities or faith and practice?
>
> What would it take to put practice first and orient your life around your faith first?

Lost

Several years ago on one of my trips to Japan I was traveling from Nagoya to Shimada and back again. It was late at night and I had only just completed my business in Shimada and so decided to stay the night there and then return to Nagoya the following day. I found a hotel near the train station, checked in and then went out in search of something to eat.

It was well after dark, and it was raining. The streets were almost empty and I was just exploring the city a little before retiring for the evening. I was walking down a side street and approaching me was a young woman who was walking with a cane for those who have vision problems. As I was approaching she called out and asked if I could help her. At this time I only had a limited command of the Japanese language and so apologized to her that I could not understand all she was saying.

She then began to speak in very good English explaining to me that she was blind and needed help finding a particular building that she had become lost and couldn't find her way. I proceeded to tell her that I was not at all familiar with the city, having just arrived earlier that day. I apologized to her that I was unable to help get her where she wanted to go. It then occurred to me that I could take her to the train station if that would help. She was extremely happy, saying that if I could get her to the train station she could then reorient herself and get where she needed to be.

As I guided her to the station we had a wonderful talk. She told me that she had been blind from birth. I asked about her ability to speak English and she told me that Americans had run the school for the blind she attended in her youth, and so they taught her English. We had a nice conversation and walk through the rainy streets. It was one of those rare moments. Here she was blind, being led by someone who did not know where he was going.

Previous to teaching the Lotus Sutra the Buddha taught expedients to lead people to the ultimate teaching of the Lotus Sutra. In many ways it was as if he were leading the blind to the train station so they could then find the way to the true complete teachings contained in the Lotus Sutra. But we need to remember that the train station is not the destination, the expedients are not the sum of the Buddha's teachings.

Do you have a spiritual mentor, companion, or community?

What serves to correct you and guide you on your path? Or do you just figure you can solo it?

Are you traveling blind; missing opportunities to improve your life?

Just A Sketch

In the "Weight of Glory", C.S. Lewis tells the story of a woman who gave birth to a son while confined as a prisoner in a dungeon. Since the boy had never seen the outside world, his mother tried to describe it by making pencil drawings. Later when they were released from prison, the simple pencil sketches were replaced by the actual images of the beautiful world.

In some ways we may think of our selves, our sufferings as being in a dungeon. In fact in Chapter 16 of the Lotus Sutra it says: "The perverted people think this world is in a great fire. The end of the kalpa of destruction is coming.'"

In other words we all too easily see the suffering and refuse to see the Buddha land that surrounds us. The Lotus Sutra in some ways provides us with a sketch of this Buddha Land, but it is up to us to actualize its appearance in our reality.

The reality of this statement, however, only exists in our individual manifestation of it in our lives. As long as we remain trapped in the view that there is only suffering, as long as we cling to this suffering as the only possible existence then we will never see the great beauty and joy that exists around us.

First we need to change ourselves. It is not possible for the reverse to happen. When we mistakenly place our happiness on the fulfillment of desires then we will always repeat the cycle of sufferings. If however we can begin to change ourselves in a fundamental way, if we change our outlook, if we change our very core of life, then slowly but surely the environment in which we live begins to change. It is not just our perception but our true self that changes which then influences the change in our surroundings.

> Who designed your reality?
>
> If you find you are doing the same things, liking the same things, talking about the same things, thinking the same things as your friends, how do you know you are leading your own life and not being lead by others?
>
> Where are you right now, is it the Buddha Land?

Life of a Pig

Ah, the life of a pig! Each new day brings nothing but slopping through the mud and snorting happily at mealtime. And what wonderful meals they have; whatever leftovers get tossed into the pen.

Sound Good? No?

This is the condition of our life, wallowing around in the dirt day after day.

As we learn in the 'Parable of the Rich Man and his Son' told in Chapter IV the son did not know the rich man was his father he had left many years before. The son did not know he was heir to great wealth and fortune.

Over many years the father gradually raised up the condition of the son, teaching him and training him in the ways of the household. Eventually as the father nears his death and the son has been successfully managing the entire fortune for the old man, the old man reveals that he is none other than the father of the young man who will now inherit the entire estate.

In this parable the rich man represents the Buddha and the poor son represents us. We are naturally endowed, with Buddhahood; it is our natural condition, yet we do not realize it. The Buddha in his compassion to make us equal to him slowly guides and instructs us thereby elevating our life to the point where we can eventually realize our innate Buddha condition.

> What sufferings have you become complacent about and no longer try to change?
>
> Are you as happy as you thought you would be 10 years ago?
>
> What can you do now to begin to change or improve?
>
> What dreams have you let go and given up on?

Your Part

Whenever we watch a play or a movie or television show most of us focus on the actors we see on screen or stage. Yet there is much more than those actors, which make the production a success. There are many other important supporting roles. There are perhaps people who began by wanting to be a part of the production but didn't want to be on stage in the spotlight. They may be the ones who change the scenery, open and close the curtains, run the lights and or cameras; maybe they assist with makeup and costumes. It might be they just clean things up, or perhaps they serve or prepare food for the crew. The success of the performance is the culmination of some intense practice dependent upon hard work and a wide range of activities.

The great oceans are made up of many single drops of water, which come together to form one body of water. This is much like both our individual practice as well as the assembly of the Sangha and makeup of a temple.

We each have our part to play and the success of the whole depends upon each person.

In our individual lives, it is the accumulating of many small efforts on a day-to-day basis that results in the accumulation of an enlightened life manifesting Buddhahood. When we look at our small efforts we may not see the potential of the accumulation of those efforts, just as we don't see the ocean in the single drop of water.

In building a Sangha or a temple it is the same. It requires the efforts of many people in order to develop a diverse and healthy vibrant Sangha or Temple. We may think that as one individual we don't matter, or we are not important. Yet when all the people come together in the collection of lives we have a rich nurturing community to practice with.

> What was and when was the last time you did something to develop and support your practice community?
>
> How might you consider supporting your Sangha to a greater degree?
>
> When was the last time you asked your Sangha what they could use from you?

Wrong Worship

What is it that we hold most important in our lives? Is it a nice house, a good car, a big paycheck, our televisions, our video games, or something else? Many people today think of prosperity as the sign of a good life, or even the benefit of their religious practice and belief.

In Buddhism we should not approach our practice as a means to increase our net worth or our social standing or material

 acquisitions. To be consumed by the increase of materialism is to be trapped in a never-ending quest, which only leads to suffering.

The quest for material gain, fueled by craving leads to suffering, or as the Buddha says: "you will be burned by them."

In the case of the Parable of the Burning house the children inside were so busy engrossed in their games, in their play, in their pursuit of happiness that they failed to notice the house was on fire and they were in great danger.

If we approach our Buddhist practice as a way to gain benefit and not as a way to become enlightened then we will continue the cycles of suffering, of getting burned. Instead we should approach Buddhism as a way to become enlightened.

The greatest benefit of practicing the Lotus Sutra is the attainment of Enlightenment equal to that of all the Buddhas, it is the end to suffering, the end to delusions.

When we become Buddhas then this land in which we live in will become the Buddha's pure land. What greater joy is there than this?

> Do you own things or do things own you?
>
> What is most important in your life, and does your life really reflect that?

Pursuit

When we want something we pursue it, and depending upon how badly we want it, we may go to great lengths to attain our goal. If we are interested in entering into a relationship with someone we may call them, and we may write notes. If we are really serious then we may ask thoughtful questions about them. We may even really want to impress them and so perhaps we take them to dinner, or the movies. We may buy them gifts, flowers, candy or other things. We will devote a lot of time and thought into how we can convince the other person how much we care for them.

If we consider our goal of attaining enlightenment how can we think that there would be any other way than to pursue it wholeheartedly, even more so than perhaps our initial efforts of wooing someone?

The opening chapter of the Lotus Sutra is full of example after example of the great efforts that individuals have gone through to attain the wisdom of the Buddha.

Many of the things those individuals practiced are no longer applicable in this age. It isn't necessary for us to practice the severe austerities those ancient practitioners engaged in. For us the single practice of chanting the Odaimoku, sacred title of the Lotus Sutra, is the most appropriate practice.

While we may not need to do the specific acts those of ancient times engaged in, we still need to consider pursuing the goal with the same amount of effort. We should consider exerting great effort as appropriate to the pursuit of enlightenment, with that practice manifesting as Namu Myoho Renge Kyo.

"...all of you present here! Understand the Dharma by faith with all your hearts!" (Lotus Sutra, Chapter II)

Though our practice is simple and seemingly easy it should not be thought that we can attain our goal without great effort. As the quote above says; "with all your hearts." Think of how we pursue something we love and cherish in our heart.

> Is the effort you put into your practice in accord with your expectation of benefit?
>
> Are there ways you could make greater effort in your Buddhist practice?

Exercise

Typically at the beginning of the New Year it is not uncommon for people to make various resolutions. One popular resolution is to improve one's health, to eat better, and to exercise regularly. I myself have a dog, and fortunately she makes me walk. But being able to take some time out and just walk allowing my mind to just be present in the moment, or to let it wander without structure is such a wonderful treat.

Of course physical exercise is important and it does have an impact on our spirit.

Why not make a resolution to exert greater effort in your Buddhist practice. Complacency has no place in Buddhism. Continuous efforts are required to fully polish our lives so that we can manifest our inherent Buddha. We should not be lulled into accepting our life, as it is no matter if it is good or not so good.

We can always improve ourselves. Polishing away the rough edges, working on the things in us that seem to pop up when faced with certain situations. Changing our response to things in our environment, which cause us suffering. There are many ways to change our spirit as we work on improving our lives. Let's exercise our body and our spirit.

> Have you given thought recently to one thing you would like to change in your life?
>
> What are your rough edges?
>
> Is there a new trait or habit you would like to incorporate into your life?

Future

It is interesting to consider predictions of the future. It seems though that predictions often made for either the coming year or the coming decade or even the coming century, more often than not are usually wrong in various, interesting and amusing ways. Frequently we wish we could see into the future so that we will know what our lives will be like.

In the Lotus Sutra the Buddha assures us our ability to attain enlightenment! Nichiren established the most efficacious manner to carry out the practice of the Lotus Sutra; chanting Odaimoku, Namu Myoho Renge Kyo, assures of manifesting our inherent Buddhahood in this very lifetime.

There are numerous predictions in the Lotus Sutra of future enlightenment of various peoples representing all the conditions of enlightenment. So no matter how we may view our present condition, the cause for enlightenment exists in this very moment within the phrase of the Sacred Title of the Lotus Sutra.

Manifesting our vow to spread the Lotus Sutra to all beings, results from our deep connection with the Lotus Sutra in previous existences. Realizing in this lifetime that our efforts will, without a doubt, result in revealing our fundamental nature of Buddha.

> How firmly do you hold onto the idea of your enlightenment?
>
> How easily do you allow yourself to settle for second best?

Longing for Home

Perhaps you have had an experience such as I had when you were young, or perhaps you know of someone who had this experience, perhaps even one of your children. My first time away from home I got homesick and I wanted to go home right away. It so happened it was while I was away one summer at camp. But there was no way that it would be possible to return home so I had to stay. Eventually the camp activities became so much fun that I soon forgot about my homesickness and when the week was over I didn't want to leave.

Have you ever set out to do something and it just got so hard you wanted to quit. I have driven across the United States many times and each time I get about half way and I think to myself I just want to go home, or I wish this trip would soon end. Perhaps you may even recall a time when you were a child and away from home for the first time and you got homesick and wanted to get back to family.

Day by day we make effort to change our life, to become enlightened, and if you're like most people you become discouraged and maybe you even want to take a break from your efforts, or even give up. Having a good friend at times like this to encourage us is without value. But practicing in and with a Sangha can provide us that lifeline. We can find a clever, or wise, or well-informed person who can understand the conditions of the road we are traveling, and encourage us.

Sometimes the problem isn't that something bad is happening or that it is hard, it may be just the opposite. Sometimes we can become sidetracked or loose our way because we have overcome an obstacle and things are now easy. We may wish to relax or coast for a while.

Times like these we really need a good friend, someone who can remind us that while we may have overcome a difficulty we still have not completed our journey to becoming enlightened. Our friend, our Sangha can help us stay focused and clear about what we have achieved and what we wish to achieve.

Looking back are you able to recall the last time you let your practice slip? Can you recall what motivated you to return to chanting and reciting the sutra?

Are you self aware enough to realize immediately when things in your life are out of balance or does it take a while?

Spoiled

Prayer in Buddhism is a somewhat different animal from the way it is frequently spoken of in other faith traditions. Prayer is about changing us and not changing something outside of ourselves. Yet, still it is not uncommon and in fact quite human to need certain things in our lives and so we may pray for them.

When we pray for things outside ourselves we must realize that we may not have our prayer answered specifically as we decide it should be. Our intent in prayer should focus on the necessary change that needs to occur in our lives so that we can attain enlightenment.

Enlightenment is the only indestructible condition of life, the gem resident inside us that allows us to exist in a constant state of happiness free from the illusions of suffering, and the illusions birth and death.

We can not get all we ask for as if we were a spoiled child able to demand of some 'super being' outside ourselves to grant our unlimited wishes. When we chant Namu Myoho Renge Kyo let us do so with great joy welling up from within our lives, with the mind of praise for the Lotus Sutra and with the desire to enable not only our own self to become enlightened but for everyone to attain enlightenment.

> What is the focus of your chanting most of the time?
>
> Are you able to chant with a single clear mind focused on meditating solely on the Odaimoku?
>
> Have you really considered chanting as a meditation and self changing activity, or is your chanting about changing things outside your being?

Playing the Part

Probably on a daily basis if you are like most people you spend some time in front of a mirror. Perhaps you look into a mirror to put on makeup or to shave, or even to model yourself checking to see if your clothes are on correctly. What do you see when you look into that mirror? Do you see your real self, and even what might be your real self.

It might be that you think that your real self is the one with the makeup on or in the fancy clothes, or you may be just the opposite and see yourself more simply. You may be a suit and tie kind of person or a blue jeans flannel shirt person. Often we find ourselves having to be something we don't think we are, or maybe we are unhappy with what we are and wish we were something else. There are many ways we may be disappointed with who we are or what we have to be.

If we take this view to heart, we realize that we are, as Bodhisattvas, assuming many different roles in this world in order to assist others, and enable them to attain enlightenment. If we look at the image reflected back at us from a mirror, and do so with the eyes of a common mortal and not with the eyes of a Buddha we may not see our true self that exists there regardless of it's manifestation.

We should not forget that as a householder, businessman, computer programmer, maintenance technician, clerk, no matter what, we are indeed playing a role. We have chosen to manifest ourselves in this life as common ordinary people who are in fact Buddhas. At the core of our life is the truth that no matter what we are Buddhas who have assumed a role in order to lead others to enlightenment.

> Have you ever thought about yourself as a Buddha?
>
> You might try looking at yourself in the mirror next time and say to the image reflected back "I am a Buddha." What does that feel like?
>
> The messages you tell yourself are the ones that get manifested in your life. Why not tell yourself good positive things?

H.U.N.T.

When an obstacle confronts us in our life we all have our individual strategies for overcoming the problem. Perhaps our strategy is successful and sometimes not, and if it is not then we may feel helpless or powerless. Recently I was reading Make More, Worry Less: Secrets from 18 Extraordinary People Who Created a Bigger Income and a Better Life by Wes Moss, in which he refers to a previous writing on the HUNT method

of overcoming obstacles. I have modified it slightly; H, harness what you have; U, Understand the nature of your problem; N, Notice your network; and T, Take the next step.

Applying wisdom to our problem can allow us to calmly look into the nature of that which is vexing us, we can see into ourselves where the roots of the problem have grown. With our Buddhist practice we can call upon the tools we have for changing ourselves and creating the causes to bring us merit. Our network is our friends in the Sangha who can help us and encourage us. Finally with the wisdom of clear understanding and chanting Odaimoku with the support of our Sangha we are prepared to take the next steps. We can take positive steps with the assurance of the Buddha that our merits will be innumerable.

Continue to practice day by day and you will see a life blossom within yourself that is transformed and free from sorrow. Become the hero of your world.

> Have you ever really considered what your personal strategy is to problem solving?
>
> Everyone has a personal strategy, even if it is random, chaotic, hapazard, and unplanned. As hard as it might be, do you think you might benefit from adopting and possibly modifying a different strategy to problem solving?

Human Being
vs.
Human Doing

Scurrying around chasing one thing after another, always trying to accomplish this or that, never resting always moving, always processing one mental challenge after another; you would think we were humandoings.

In our Buddhist practice we are truly on a spiritual journey. Daily as we chant Odaimoku and recite the Sutra, we are making the causes to create the necessary balance in our lives between being and doing. Some view Buddhism as merely a self-help process, practicing mindfulness as if that was all there is. If we view our Buddhist practice in such a way then we are still residing in the realm of doing, even if the doing is more beneficial than other doings.

As a self-help model alone we would be merely replacing one method of doing with another method. Buddhism offers more, much more. Buddhism creates the conditions within our lives for a transcendent experience of our relationship not only to and with ourselves but also being transcendent with all else.

Finding our true identity is key, and we can't do this if we ignore the being part of human. Daily we work hard and worry, yet the gem we truly seek is something we already posses.

> Are you a humandoing or a humanbeing?
>
> Is Buddhism one more thing you have brought into your life to do? Rather than to be?
>
> Are you able to realize when you are doing versus when you could be being?

Perfect Fit

The Bodhisattvas that arose from beneath the ground are none other than ourselves, if we open ourselves up to realizing it. But the realization is not just a mental acceptance of such information, it is deeper, it occurs on a different plane from intellect. In order to be those Bodhisattvas we need to manifest that condition, draw it out of who and what we are in this life. There are not two separate entities, self and Bodhisattva from beneath the earth, however it is up to us to unify them in body and mind, in action and in word.

When we go to apply for a job we are frequently asked what our qualifications are, what skills do we have that would make us suitable for the position. We may have gone to school, or we may bring some experiences from past jobs. We may also have some innate ability, which will be valuable as we work. And it isn't just applying for a job that the issue of skills comes up.

We may even at times ask ourselves whether or not we have the necessary ability to be Bodhisattvas from under the ground.

Such were the questions asked of the Buddha, not unlike questions we may ask ourselves trying to figure out if we could possibly be these great Bodhisattvas. Yet we should have no doubts that there is no one more qualified or capable to carry out the difficult work of spreading the Lotus Sutra as Bodhisattvas in this later age.

> Thinking about the idea of going to work at new job. While you probably had many skills to do the work already, were there not also many new things you had to learn?
>
> You have the necessary innate ability of Bodhisattva even while at the same time needing to polish and learn some, as well as possibly unlearn some things.
>
> Can you identify one thing in your life you may frequently overlook that is indeed a good characteristic?

Walking

Walking is good for you. Of course you probably already know that, so I'm not telling you anything new. But did you know it is good for your Buddhist practice leading to enlightenment?

By adding walking to your daily activity you can increase your cardio vascular health allowing your body to work better. When we meditate we practice breathing in deeply and exhaling completely. When we do this we are actually purifying our blood by allowing more oxygenated air into our

blood and exhaling more toxins from our body. When we walk we do the same things.

Walking can also help to reduce the threat of diabetes, and reduce your weight. Walking can promote mindfulness especially when we walk with a clear mind, opening up to the sights and sounds around us; this is one reason I prefer to walk without listening to any music.

In the Lotus Sutra we learn of Medicine-King Bodhisattva: "He walked about the world, seeking Buddhahood strenuously with all his heart for twelve thousand years until at last he obtained the samadhi by which he could transform himself into any other living being.' Having obtained this samadhi, he had great joy." - Lotus Sutra, Chapter XXVIII

Something you might try when you are walking is chanting Odaimoku either silently in your mind or even vocalizing it. When you walk say Namu on the left foot, then alternate each foot with Myo on right, Ho on left, Ren on right, Ge on left, Kyo on right. Now you are back to the left foot and Namu.

> Can you think of other areas of your life where you could merge your practice into ordinary activities?
>
> If you named several it might be beneficial if you only picked one to do rather than trying to do many.
>
> Perhaps put a reminder on your calendar to check in with yourself in a week to see how successful you were in implementing the change. If you weren't so successful try again.

Sandcastles

We may have had an experience of building sandcastles while on vacation at some beach. Sandcastles are not very long lasting, usually until the next tide cycle, and then it is gone.

Sandcastles are a fun way to spend some relaxing time. Yet how much of our lives do we spend constructing sandcastles in our everyday lives. We make castles of stuff, basking in our accomplishments. We build mighty fortresses out of our sense of self and rightness. We build walls of superiority and arrogance to ward off the connections of life and the world around us. We go to great lengths doing what seems worthwhile and important, yet in the end it is worthless. And can easily be destroyed by the changes in life, be it job, relationships, income, health, even aging.

The reality of impermanence and the truth of change is relentless at tearing down our sandcastle walls. Only when we awaken to the true nature of reality, the Buddhahood that perfectly exists already in our life can we experience a life of indestructible happiness.

Chanting Odaimoku and reciting the Lotus Sutra, can bring about the awakening to our true selves. As we practice the eight-fold path and chant Odaimoku we can make the necessary changes in our view and our existence to ensure overcoming any obstacle. There is no safety or protection residing in a sandcastle.

How skillful are you at avoiding deep connections with others around you?

Do you frequently find yourself depersonalizing others, even with a simple statement such as "that person..."? Discounting the other person's emotions or feelings?

Do you think about connectedness with the cashiers and service people in your life, or on your job? Or are they just fixtures?

What Song Are You Singing

Music plays a big part in our everyday lives, even in ways we may not realize. I know my day always seems brighter and lighter when I have some music on, most of the time classical music. I don't have a television anymore so I can't say for sure, but music used to be a big part of selling products; if a product had a catchy jingle then you were sure to remember it easily.

Frequently songs are written to convey a particular message; sometimes a message that could not otherwise be told. I think of some of the protest songs of the sixties or even back to union organizing times. One chilling example is the song "Strange Fruit" which sings of the lynching's that took place in the south, the hangings of African-Americans.

Not all songs are sad, many and probably most are happy and uplifting. Songs are sung by children to help them remember lessons. Think of the ABC song and how it helps sing the letters of the alphabet.

Songs frequently are written to celebrate a special occasion. You don't have to go long in classical music or even religious music before you come across pieces that were written for a coronation or another event or for certain spiritual circumstances.

In Buddhism music has played an important role as well, even though today it seems greatly diminished. Today Buddhism is not so much known for music, and yet it is at the heart of Buddhism. The original sutras were probably taught and memorized in some music or poetic fashion.

In the services we perform at the temple there are various songs, called Shomyo that are sung in celebration during the service.

What kind of music do you sing with your heart? What is your song of the day, the song of your life?

When we chant the Odaimoku we are on one hand meditatively engaging in the recitation of the Sacred Title of the Lotus Sutra, we are also singing our praise of the teachings of the Buddha, which it contains. The greatest song we can sing is the Odaimoku that comes from joy within our lives.

When we can chant with great joy, a joy that wells up from within then our entire life becomes a song. Our life can touch other's lives through the beautiful music that is our unique life.

> Is there a song you can identify that ether sums up your Buddhist practice or reminds you of your practice?
>
> There may not be one, but is there a song that could remind you of the time when you first began to practice?
>
> Can you recall your first introduction to Nichiren Buddhism?

Gutters and Windows

A sign, spotless white with very neat red lettering sits in front of a house. The sign advertises "Gutters & Windows – Quality Work Guaranteed." The sign, however sits in stark contrast with the house behind it; the sign being pristine, while the house behind it is in a state of complete disrepair. The house with its paint peeling, the windows cracked and broken, and no gutters calls into question what the sign was really advertising.

Thinking about the contrast between the sign being pristine and the house behind it in disrepair I wonder how often our lives present such a stark contrast. How often do we espouse or claim we are Buddhists and yet we live day to day in the decaying building of the triple world and we show no positive effect of our Buddhist practice to others.

Is there a disconnect between the sign claiming Buddhism, and the manifest reality of our lives? Do we make every effort to put a good front on Buddhism or are we complacent as we carry out our daily activities? Are we setting a good example of being capable of leading others out of their crumbling house in the triple world?

We can be as the Tathagatas and show our friends many examples of how with our Buddhist practice we can repair and become happy in the triple world. Let us renew our efforts to practice with joy, live with joy, and interact with joy. Lets all manifest and bring into reality the Buddha land in our lives.

> Are there times when you catch yourself not behaving as a Buddhist or not living as a Buddha?
>
> Wearing a wrist mala, or wrist beads could serve to remind you to reconsider certain behaviors?
>
> Are there other ways you can provide visual cues to yourself to remember to be a Buddhist?

Potato Chips

It used to be that there was only one kind of potato chip, that is one kind sold by many different companies. Now however you go to the store and there are lots and lots of choices for chips in a bag. Amazing isn't it.

I used to try to make potato chips at home for my partner. Time after time I tried and they just never came out anything like the chips you could get in the bag. The bag chip was his favorite kind, but I tried none-the-less.

At one time I worked right next to a deli and the guy who owned it made his own chips every day. So I asked him what the secret was to making chips. He told me it was the soaking in water. You have to soak them in water to remove all the starch from the slices. Who would have thought? I had tried adjusting the thickness of the slice, the oil, the heat, the pan, all kinds of things I tried. I never knew soaking in water that was the key ingredient.

You know how you feel when you stumble on a solution to a problem you have been trying to solve for a long time. You get so excited, or at least I do. Well in our lives we have been trying to solve the problem of how to be happy. What does it take to be happy, we may ask ourselves?

The Buddha in a previous life sought out the Lotus Sutra, and when he came upon someone to teach it to him he was so happy he served that person in various personal ways. He would fetch water, and food and do household chores; all sorts of things in order to hear the Dharma of the Lotus Flower Sutra. This was the relationship between Shakyamuni and Devadatta in a previous lifetime.

Here in this life we have come upon the Lotus Sutra, even though many of us didn't actually seek it directly. We probably came across it by accident. As we practice we gain joy in our lives, we are able to overcome various obstacles, and begin to make changes to manifest Buddhahood. Chanting Odaimoku is so simple. It is like soaking the potatoes in water to remove the starch; we need to soak our lives in the Odaimoku of the Lotus Sutra to remove the things that hold us back from enlightenment.

Serving the Lotus Sutra as above and chanting Odaimoku is the best way to become enlightened, like soaking potatoes in water is the best way to make potato chips.

> What limitations do you have to fully practicing the Lotus Sutra?
>
> What limitations do you have to supporting your Sangha?
>
> What limitations do you have to making donations to the Lotus Sutra?

Whom To Ask

This has probably never happened to you before, but the other day I was out doing some shopping and couldn't find what I was looking for. I approached someone to ask if they knew where the item was located. They turned around and I immediately realized they didn't work in the store they were a customer. They said they couldn't help me, and so I proceeded to try to find someone who could help me find what I was looking for.

Herein lies the rub, finding the right person to ask. In Buddhism today we have many sources to go to for answers to our questions. We may think that since there is so much information available to us that we can simply discover the answer on our own. We may be lulled into thinking that with our ever so clever mind, and our remarkably reliable abilities, that we can perfectly piece together an amazing answer. Tempting isn't it?

Yet, how sure can we be that we are seeking the answer to the correct question while at the same time asking the correct source? Frequently magicians in a book I am reading for leisure respond; 'It's complicated.'

Having good friends in a Sangha and a reliable teacher can

help us fact-check our assumptions and conclusions; just as the Sangha at the time of the Buddha went to Manjusri.

Going to some skilled person to see what they have learned and what they have experienced can be a great aid in our practice of Buddhism. Yes, we ultimately have to personally absorb and inculcate into our own lives the truth of the matter, but having a good friend, a Sangha support, a teacher can help us to navigate the storehouse of treasures of Buddhism.

> Do you always ask yourself the right questions?
>
> Do you limit the answers you are willing to accept, avoiding the uncomfortable ones, the inconvenient ones, or the difficult ones?

Goldilocks

I suppose we are all somewhat familiar with the story of Goldilocks. The gist of the story is that first there was one thing that didn't satisfy Goldilocks at first. Having three choices of that thing she then picked the one that seemed just right for her. Then there was another thing of which she had three varying options and again she chose the one that seemed just right for her. Several times she did this until finally she falls asleep comfortable in a bed that seemed just right for her.

This all sounds pretty pleasant. If only life were that simple, right? I heard a story a while back on the radio about a guy who has been on a quest to find just the right couch for his house. He has spent many many years on this quest. He has traveled to various places to find just the right couch. His

efforts have not yet yielded the so call perfect couch. He has even spent large sums of money on couches thinking they would be the perfect one, sums that could buy a whole house full of furniture, and yet never the perfect Goldilocks couch for him.

Prior to the Lotus Sutra, the Buddha taught many different teachings for a variety of people; teachings well suited to the capacities and natures of those he taught. With the teaching of the Lotus Sutra though, we have the advent of the unification of all those individual teachings into one specific complete teaching that goes beyond the ending point of the parts of the whole.

Our challenge, as contemporary practitioners of Buddhism, is to learn from the prior teachings, but do so from the point of the unity presented in the Lotus Sutra. Our challenge is also to learn to master all the constituent parts of the whole of our personal being. We may think that simply following something that is convenient or a Goldilocks teaching is what we want, but just as the elders of the Sangha express, it may not actually be what we need.

When a complete teaching replaces an incomplete teaching it is necessary to move to understanding and embracing the complete. Just as the elders of the Sangha realized in the Lotus Sutra.

> Is it easy for you to avoid things that cause you to feel uncomfortable, or require too much effort?
>
> Do you have a mix and match approach to your spiritual life, avoiding commitment and choosing the convenient path?

Yoda

"If no mistake have you made, yet losing you are ... a different game you should play." Yoda from Star Wars

I am not sure about you; you probably haven't done some things over and over with the same results and become frustrated as I have. There have been times when I'll do something, get a result I don't like or expect and then try again. Sometimes I may try over and over doing exactly the same thing and always getting the same result that I don't want.

"Insanity: Doing the same thing over and over again and expecting different results." Albert Einstein

So day after day, lifetime after lifetime, and birth after birth we repeat the cycles of birth, sickness, old age, and death. The four sufferings haunt us, and we try every strategy to eliminate them from our lives. If not our own sufferings we suffer the sickness and death of friends and loved ones. We suffer the attachment to things that are impermanent. We suffer the illusions that we are independent of the things that exist outside ourselves.

I like the phrase, 'They are trying to stop suffering by suffering" from Chapter 2 in the Lotus Sutra. How easy it is to keep doing the easy thing, the thing that has not worked well for us in the past? Buddhism requires us to change, to challenge, to delve deep into our inner most being to try to understand both what

is good and beneficial for us and what keeps us from doing that very thing. As long as we keep ignoring the obvious, our suffering, our thinking that there is no other way, we will continue to suffer. Ignorance is one of the three poisons; ignorance traps us in a cycle of ignorance and suffering.

> Is there anything in your life you do that keeps yielding the same unwanted effect?
>
> What are some changes in your life you avoid making?

If Necessary, Use Words

Roughly 2500 or so years ago the Buddha taught the Lotus Sutra. It becomes apparent about halfway through that the Buddha considers, at least on one level, that this teaching is not so much for his contemporary disciples but for people in the time after the Buddha's death.

We learn, as the sutra progresses, that of all the folks gathered at Mount Sacred Eagle for the preaching of the Lotus Sutra were not the people the Buddha actually had in mind to carry out the continuation of his legacy as laid out in the Lotus Sutra.

As practitioners of the Lotus Sutra in the Later Age we have made a pledge to transmit the teachings of the Buddha contained in the Lotus Sutra.

Ok, we all know the story, we all know what we are supposed to do, right? The big question then becomes, just exactly how should we go about accomplishing our mission? How do we transmit this sutra in this time so far removed from the Buddha?

"Preach the gospel everyday; if necessary, use words." (St. Francis of Assisi

Here is the heart of the matter. Every day we should live our lives as not just disciples of the Buddha, but as Bodhisattvas from beneath the ground, disciples of the Eternal Buddha. Our actions are the most powerful form of speech.

> Have you ever considered that your actions actually are a form of propagation?
>
> Is there one thing you could do which would bring your actions more in line with your beliefs?
>
> How about making a month long goal to track your changes?

Slinkys And Marbles

Not sure if you remember or even played with Slinkys or marbles: do children now a days play with such simple toys? The thing about the older toys was that they were not self propelled and didn't rely on batteries or electronics. In the case of the slinky, a coiled wire or plastic spring, you could get it to do things but you had to assist it from its static still state.

Of course marbles needed a hand too. They didn't move unless you supplied some energy to get them going.

Buddhism is much the same way. The at rest or static state of Buddhism is not existent. Buddhism is by its very nature a state of constant effort. If you are standing still, you are falling behind. Buddhism requires constant effort, daily and moment-by-moment effort to make the changes in our lives through practice so that we can attain enlightenment.

This statement can be read from two points of view. One, it is difficult to see or observe a Buddha separate from us. The other view is that it is difficult to see or observe the Buddha in us. At any rate, as the sutra says it is difficult and we should make efforts with all our hearts.

I like that it says hearts, because I think that we need to have a passion and joy that resides in our heart to really get the most out of our practice. If we are doing merely as an obligation expecting that if we do enough penance then we will achieve some thing then I am not sure of the results.

We may get tired or discouraged along the way, but remember the story of the magic city.

The Buddha assures us, we have his promise that we cannot fail if we continue to exert ourselves.

If we continue to practice the Lotus Sutra we can establish within our lives the indestructible condition of enlightenment just as we are.

> Examining your life, are there areas where you might be able to generate more excitement in your practice?
>
> Do you find it easier to practice Buddhism standing still?
>
> Do you notice as many changes in your life when you do nothing as opposed to when you make great effort?

Genuine Friends

Tracking the changing vocabulary of English the folks at New Oxford American Dictionary decided that the word of the year in 2009 would be unfriend. They define it as a verb, "to remove someone as a friend on a social networking web site," such as Facebook. As you probably know, on that site, Friends allow each other to access their personal information. They may have never met face to face or even really know each other and may only be remotely aware of who each is. They may not even exchange any personal greetings online. In our world of fleeting cyber acquaintances, we may be drifting away from close connections of true friends.

Friends form a unique relationship; true friendship is one of mutual commitment to the well being of the other. Friendship takes time to build, it takes trust, openness, and a desire to put in to it freely just for the benefit of the other, and not just what can be taken away. And from a Buddhist perspective a good Buddhist friend can help us to maintain our practice, a person who will tell us when we have done something right

or when we might do something better. A good Buddhist friend will not merely say things just to make us feel good; instead they will say things to us that will make us be good. This is also the kind of friend we can become to others; helping them attain Buddhahood is the best gift we can give to our friends.

Sometimes we may need to be encouraged and sometimes we may need to be corrected in order to see the gem that is buried in our lives. In all cases do not be discouraged, learn what there is to learn, and gradually you will be able to extract the gem of enlightenment and reveal it in your life. The Buddha never 'unfriends' us, nor should we.

Is your circle of friends growing or shrinking? Online friends versus real time friends?

How many of your friends are Buddhist?

How many of your friends support your Buddhist practice and to whom you can share your experiences?

Reconciliation And Forgiveness

There are many traditions associated with the start of the Chinese New Year, which we do not have in our western celebrations. One such tradition is to reconcile and forget all grudges and to wish peace and happiness for all. In the west we do offer well wishes for the coming year, but we don't often speak of reconciling and forgetting past grudges. This idea is worthy of considering every day and not limited to only the beginning of a New Year.

The way we begin the New Year, the way we begin any activity is a strong influence on how the future will unfold. Doing a thorough cleaning of one's house is also a tradition at the start of the Chinese New Year. This makes sense, after all why would we want to begin anew with dirt and clutter either in our house or in our lives.

There is a ritual that we sometimes observe in Nichiren Shu called suigyo, or water purification practice. The phrases we recite as we are performing this ritual speak of cleansing ourselves, making our lives pure in order to carry out the practice of spreading the Dharma.

Let us renew our efforts to clean ourselves, not only physically but spiritually as well. Let us reconcile all of our past grudges, the things that hold us back, let us make fresh our entire lives, and renew our efforts to share the Dharma with great joy.

Thinking of today being the first day of the rest of your life call to mind one person you would like to work on forgiving.

Again, also think of one regret you would like to let go.

Finally, think of one grudge to wipe away.

Falling From The Tree

My father used to tell me that the seeds of a magnolia tree will not germinate under the parent tree. If you think about most other trees such as oak, maple, pecan, pine and many others their seeds will take root under the parent tree. If you look at a magnolia they can spread out quite wide, the leaves are very large and thick and they fall to the ground almost all year long. I wonder if perhaps because of evolution seeds naturally selected themselves to only germinate outside the boughs of the parent tree, because it would be extremely difficult to

germinate under the large thick leaf cover around the base of the tree.

At any rate it is interesting to think about, or at least to me it is interesting.

In the Lotus Sutra the chapter on Simile of Herbs points out that while it is true that there are various kinds of plants, each with its own unique characteristics the cloud of rain provides nourishment to them all in the necessary quantities even though some need more and others need less.

The beauty of the teachings of the Buddha is regardless of what our unique capability is, what our unique gifts may be, or even what our handicaps are we all can equally benefit from the teachings of the Buddha. Buddhism and enlightenment are not dependent upon how clever, what our economic status is, what our gender is, it doesn't matter. None of the differences we may use to label and separate each other, those labels do not apply when it comes to benefiting from the teaching and practice of Buddhism.

> How much thought have you given to what you are good at and what you are not?
>
> Do you practice sticking to your boundaries and striving to do those things that nourish you versus things that drain your spirit?

Degrees Of Separation

The Hungarian author Frigyes Karinthy wrote a short story he called "Chain-Links," in which he proposed the idea that any two individuals in the world are connected through, at most, five acquaintances. The idea was revived later and is now known as "Six Degrees of Separation." Whether or not it is completely true that we are in fact only separated from each other by no more than five acquaintances, the fact remains that we are interconnected in many various, interesting and sometimes intriguing ways. Consider even for a moment the number of people you are connected to that you do not even know; important but unknown to you are the people who half a world away drill, pump and ship the crude oil that becomes the gasoline for your car or bus. Consider only half a continent away the farmer who produces the strawberries you enjoy out of season, or any of the other varieties of foods that used to not be available when they didn't grow in our own neighborhoods.

Our connections, our dependence on large numbers of people we do not know personally has expanded tremendously in the more than eighty yeas since Karinthy wrote his story. These are people we may not know personally but whom we are directly tied to.

As we benefit from the efforts of countless unnamed people from all over the globe, so to can they benefit from our seemingly insignificant effort of sharing the Dharma with even only one friend or contact in our lives.

> Practice mindful connections by trying to of all the people who had a hand in getting to you your food.
>
> Before you bite into your next meal take a moment to consider the many unknown but essential people responsible for your meal.

The Dance

The Lotus Sutra mentions dancing as both an expression of joy as well as something to be offered in appreciation for the Dharma. I was thinking about this, as I especially like the images that come to mind when it talks about people dancing with great joy.

When a person dances are they tying to get somewhere? There isn't really a destination in mind for the purpose of dancing. The goal of dancing isn't to get from this place to the next. When we dance it is the joy of the steps. It is the pleasure even possibly from not needing to go anywhere but to just enjoy the process.

Dancing as an expression of joy I think is more joyful if we just enjoy the process. And as an expression of joy it can also be an

expression of appreciation for the joy in our lives and for the Dharma. An expression of appreciation then becomes gratitude arising from joy.

Our practice is much like dancing in many ways. Our practice while certainly directed towards enlightenment is most importantly about the steps along the way and the joy of those steps, which actually manifest in the dance of and not to enlightenment.

> See if you can form an image in your mind of someone dancing for joy. Now see if you can insert yourself into that image.
>
> When you chant is it Odaimoku that is dancing for joy or is it driven by needs and desires unfulfilled?

Lion And Fox

Lions are the so-called kings of the jungle; they are fierce hunters. Foxes are known for their cleverness; they are very capable of avoiding the hunter. The lion is good at what it does; the fox is good at what it does. Each has skills suited to its survival or maybe the skills developed because of what it needed to become to survive.

It is like the German proverb, which says; "what the lion cannot manage to do the fox can."

Sometimes we think of Buddhism and think we need to be just like the Buddha. We may even think that we need to sit under a tree and be peaceful like we imagine the Buddha. But I think we miss the point sometimes by wishing to become exactly like the Buddha and fail to realize our goal is to attain enlightenment just as we are.

There are many things that we can do that the Buddha could not, just as there were things the Buddha could do that we can't. The Buddha was not a computer programmer, nor an investment banker, nor a grocery store clerk, nor any number of countless other jobs we must engage in.

The Buddha doesn't teach us to abandon those things but to excel in them, as the Buddha would do. We can become enlightened and still do the seemingly ordinary things we do everyday and be Buddhas doing them.

Become enlightened as the Buddha was.

> Do you ever think about enlightenment being possible on your job?
>
> Consider the fact that of all the Buddha's life most of it was walking and teaching. Consider where you spend the bulk of your time, now think of how you can be a Buddha there.

Sculpture

It is said that Michelangelo once replied, when asked how he created such beautiful sculptures, that all you had to do was carve away the stuff you didn't want. Of course! Now I understand! It should be very easy to sculpt with that kind of instruction.

Every day we are the sculptor of our day and lives. What we decide to chip away and what we decide to leave will determine how our day sculpture looks.

When we think of carving an image of the Buddha I suspect that generally we think in terms of taking some material and simply carving a Buddha. But if we think about this in terms of our lives and sculpting our day and lives we can see another meaning to this.

If we want ourselves to be like the Buddha, an image of the Buddha, we need to carve it out of our lives. Every day, slowly and carefully, chipping away at all the things in our lives that are keeping us from being Buddhas.

> Think of one thing to chip away that would improve your personal life sculpture.
>
> Now set a goal to consistently work for an extended period of time on just that one thing.

Empty Cup

Frequently in Buddhism teachers and others will use the analogy of emptying the teacup. It is a good image when you consider that before you can receive more tea, fresh tea, hot tea, different tea you need to first empty your cup. If your cup remains full then there is no space for more.

The same goes with our lives. If we cling tightly to what we have and do not seek to give it away then we have no space for more. If we are feeling good and have received merit from our practice of Buddhism what good does it do us to cling tightly? Just as if we hold the tea in the cup it becomes stale, cold, and bitter, so too if we hold on to our merit, our joy.

By giving to others we make space within our lives for more. By sharing with others our joy of Buddhist practice, by encouraging others to never give up, by sharing our material as well as spiritual gains we make space for being refilled, being refreshed.

We may think that if we give it away there will be an empty spot, but the nature of life is that the empty spot will not remain empty as long as we make space for compassion and caring for others.

We may become tired and we may have to rest, but if we truly can give with great joy we will be replenished and recharged and able to continue on.

"I am not tired of giving the rain of the Dharma to all living beings." (Lotus Sutra, Chapter V)

> Another way to consider the full tea cup is in our study of Buddhism. Do you ever find yourself saying "I already know that" or "I already understand that" and then seek no further for deeper understanding.
>
> When was the last time you review the basics of Buddhist belief, setting aside what you already know?
>
> Why not take some time and go back and review and seek for deeper understanding?

Change Us

At night my dog likes to sleep in my bed. Isn't it amazing how the littlest dogs can take up the most amount of space? They may enjoy sleeping in bed but they sure don't get the concept of sharing. It is comforting to have my dog curled up at the foot of the bed. And in our case if she takes up too much room I just put my feet on top of her or my leg, this dog doesn't seem to mind.

Several times a night though she'll come up to the head of the bed and paw at the covers hoping that I'll let her climb underneath. I usually don't, because it gets too hot after a while and then she wants out and when she does she pulls all the covers off me. Sometimes though she'll paw and paw at the covers, insisting I let her under. She'll go to first my face side and paw and if she has no luck she'll climb over me and paw at the backside. Then she'll climb back over and do it all again.

Without even realizing it we live our lives sometimes just like my puppy looks for comfort under the warm blanket. We travel through existence after existence, through suffering after suffering going from one desire to another or from one way to trying to fulfill a fleeting desire to a different way, always to no avail.

One of the reasons we fail is because we have not clearly understood what it is that we are truly seeking. We think that if we change this one condition or another or if we were in a different situation we would be happier. We fail to understand that the condition of Buddhahood, the condition of our indestructible and complete end to suffering exists within us already.

Some situations aren't meant for us to change, they are meant to change us.

> When faced with a challenge in your life what do you tend to do first; figure out how to change it or figure out how to change yourself?
>
> Think of a current challenge facing you. Try looking at this challenge in a new way and see if there is something about you that changing might solve the problem.

Questions

I have a friend who has recently welcomed a new baby into his family. I myself have never had children, but I can imagine it is a pretty exciting thing. I frequently see parents out in the neighborhood, as I walk around with my puppy, out walking with their young children. Children are amazing things aren't they? Just imagine where we would be without children.

Parents who have children or even folks who have raised pets from early birth understand something about questions and inquisitiveness. Good teachers understand this as well. The key to learning and perhaps the first requirement to real learning is questioning and being inquisitive. Yes, we can force something on someone and try to make them learn something but the real learning the deeply embraced learning comes when the learner has an excitement to learn what is being taught. Children come with this automatically built in.

Examining the teachings of the Buddha we see that the Buddha frequently waits until he is asked a question before he teaches. In fact our Buddhist practice really doesn't begin to take place until we ourselves ask and prepare for the answer to the question of how to end suffering.

It isn't until we become aware that we suffer, or that there might be an alternative to suffering do we begin to even look for a way to end suffering. When we awaken to the truth about suffering being an option we begin to ask questions about how to end it, how to practice Buddhism.

All we have to do is to seek out the answer. If however we only do so from a merely intellectual perspective, thinking that the acquisition of more knowledge, will solve the problem then we have not embraced the heart of being inquisitive. Think again of the child who when very young really is looking not just for the answer to a question but an understanding of the complete nature of the object or thought.

So too, we need to delve deep into the nature of our suffering and the way to eliminate it, always seeking. "The Buddha will remove any doubt of those who seek the teaching of the Three Vehicles. No question will be left unresolved." (Lotus Sutra, Chapter I)

> How difficult is it for you to examine your life?
>
> When you do self-examination do you look for evidence to support your conclusions?
>
> Are your conclusions general in nature or are they specific?
>
> Frequently people will say general statements about themselves, which are not based upon facts. A person might say I am a terrible person when in fact they are ignoring much about themselves that is indeed quite good. In self-examination, stick to the facts support by evidence and avoid generalities.

It's Your Choice

A few years ago I was helping a Japanese exchange student as he settled in to life here in the United States. He asked me if I would take him to a store to purchase some basic necessities. Without giving it any thought I took him to one of our larger department stores. He asked me to show him where the shampoo was located and so I took him over to that area. I showed him a whole long row floor to 6 foot high selection of shampoo. He turned to me flabbergasted and asked how do I know which one to pick.

We probably think nothing of having a choice of probably close to a hundred different kinds of shampoo, but for most people in the world the choice may be limited to only a couple dozen or less selections. Our society has become one where we assume we can have an almost customized experience. We have come to expect that we can pick and choose among a variety of selections. We want things our way.

In spite of the fog created by the appearance of multiple choices for everything in our life, there really is one fundamental choice that we need to make and often ignore. That choice is the choice of whether or not to be happy.

The Buddha has given us the ultimate teaching, the purpose for the existence of all Buddhas, the treasure-store of teachings. It is our choice whether or not we will take advantage of it, pick it up, and embrace it , and choose to be happy.

> Are the choices you make consistent with the outcomes you wish for your enlightenment? Always? Frequently? Occasionally?
>
> When making life decisions do you avoid the difficult options and select only the easy ones?
>
> In your spiritual practice how much of it is about doing only the things you like and not also engaging in practices you don't like? Picking the easy way?

Going Through

Winston Churchill said: "If you're going through hell, keep going"

Makes sense to me. There isn't much point in stopping I hell, not if you can keep going and get out.

The trick is to know and realize that we are in hell, since sometimes we are not even aware that we are suffering. I think many of us become so acquainted with sufferings that we just think it is a normal part of our lives and there is nothing to do about it.

Yet, as we learn in Buddhism, that doesn't have to be the case. We can wake up from our anesthetized state, a state

of almost being immune to the effects or feelings of suffering and begin to move on through.

For others they may recognize they are in the hell of suffering but are so lost they do not know how to move, or even if there is any way to go forward to end the suffering.

To those walking their path of suffering and who become tired or discouraged the teachings of the Buddha offer a way out, a way to continue, a way to end the suffering.

We only need to embrace the teachings of the Buddha.

> Are there areas of your life where you have accepted suffering as a fact and unavoidable, and so have stopped looking for ways to eliminate the suffering?
>
> Remember, fundamentally suffering is a choice of your response and your outlook. Pain is a fact suffering optional.

Learning

Here in the United Sates people are known to say that two things in life are guaranteed, death and taxes. Thinking about this I am struck by the fact that learning is not one of the two, nor is it a third. It is true, though, that learning isn't promised. There is no certainty that we will learn. It is a choice we make; to learn or not to learn.

Just as learning is not mandatory, nor is it promised to us, neither is survival. We don't have to learn as we go through life; we can choose to continue to do the same things over and over never change. We also have the same correlational option for survival. We tend to survive in relationship to how well we learn in life.

Learning the facts of wisdom of life is as important as learning the facts of life. It is not enough to know what words mean, it is important to know how to use the words. It isn't sufficient to learn numbers but to learn how to employ the numbers. It is true in everything; we learn the facts but we need to learn how to use those facts in skillful ways, in productive ways, in ways that enhance not only our lives but also the lives of others.

In Buddhism it helps to learn as much as we can, that way we are better prepared as the Sutra says, to answer questions skillfully, to answer not only the questions of others, but our own questions as well. Yet, perhaps as important if not possible more so is the requirement that we learn how to use the knowledge of Buddhism in our lives in both practical and useful ways; in other words to bring the wisdom of the Buddha into existence in our life.

> Is there a disconnect in your life between what you know and your ability or willingness to use knowledge in beneficial ways?
>
> In Buddhism how much of what you know is actually what you do?

Opportunity

Throughout our lives we are presented with opportunities continuously. There are opportunities presented to us in every moment of our existence.

"A man who misses his opportunity, and a monkey who misses his branch cannot be saved." Hindu proverb

When you consider the many opportunities we have had to practice any number of other religions other than Buddhism we can appreciate how rare the chance we were presented with. Buddhism is not the most common religion in America. I have heard that Buddhism is the fourth major religion in America, yet it is still rare to come into contact with Buddhism, especially in some areas of the country.

The two princes in chapter XXVII of the Lotus Sutra realized what a rare gift they had been given to meet the Buddha. If you have a copy of the Lotus Sutra you might enjoy refreshing your memory of Chapter XXVII.

The choice has been presented to us; we have been given a wonderful and rare opportunity. Now, do we miss this chance, will we be like the monkey who misses his branch as he swings through the forest? There is no saving either the monkey who misses his branch, nor the person who misses the opportunity to practice the Lotus Sutra when given the option to do so. The branch presents itself, the Lotus Sutra presents itself, but it is up to us just as it is up to the monkey whether or not we reach out and hold fast.

> How closely in touch are you with a sense of gratitude and appreciation for the Lotus Sutra in your life?
>
> How closely in touch are you with gratitude for all of the comforts and gifts of your life?
>
> How easy is it for you to express your gratitude to others?

Building

In the neighborhood where I live, right behind the temple they are tearing down numerous houses. The removal of these dwellings is for the purpose of reclaiming flood plain areas along a creek. It is amazing that I can walk by one day and a house is standing intact and then the next day it is a pile of rubble. By the third day it is all cleared and by day four it has been seeded over and there remains no evidence of a building ever having been there.

It is also noteworthy that it only takes a couple of people to accomplish all this. When we contrast this with the amount

of effort it takes to build a house it is really striking. It takes many men with a variety of skills several days, if not weeks or months, to build a house. Then it takes more crews of men to come in and do the finishing work, such as wiring, plumbing, and so forth. Finally more people come in to do the painting and carpeting and other such projects. All of this takes a lot of skilled labor, a lot of time, and planning. Yet to tear down that same structure takes only a few hours.

We cannot expect our practice of Buddhism, wishing to become enlightened, to take a short period of time, or little effort. Yet we can destroy all that we have attained all that we have accomplished within a short period of time by being discouraged and abandoning our practice.

> Are you committed to doing the necessary work to attain enlightenment?
>
> When failing at accomplishing something are you equally able to blame the effort as you are to blame the process?
>
> If for example you go to the doctor and he gives you instructions to change things in your life in order to improve your health and you don't follow his advice. Which person is at fault?

Drains to Creek

In the neighborhood where the temple is located and in fact in most of the city you see signs on almost all the drains in the roads along the cubs that warn about dumping. This is because all the street drains go directly into the creek system that is a natural part of the area.

If pollution or other debris enters these drains then it goes directly into the natural water eco system of our city. There has been a particularly concerted effort in the past few years to actually reclaim some of the natural creeks in this city even to the extent of removing high-rise buildings and shopping centers. These reclaimed stream beads are being beautified as well as being restored to as natural a condition as is possible after a hundred or more years of neglect.

Because of this effort the natural waterways and tributaries in this city are much healthier and support a much more diverse population of wild life than ever in recent years. So naturally since so much effort has been put into the restoration it would be counter productive to have waste enter these streams through the storm drainage system.

The efforts to restore the natural water environment in the city have lead to other parkway and greenway projects, which have also contributed to the overall beauty and livability of the city.

Sometimes uncovering or showing a small part of something enables us to see the potential of something even greater. Protecting something that is small or encouraging a fledgling effort can result in unimaginable outcomes. As our lives are slowly freed from illusions and then our eyes purified we are able to see the truth in the sutra, the truth in our lives and become Buddhas.

> It might be eye opening for you to actually make a list of improvements in your life, both big and small, since you began practicing Buddhism.
>
> Are there things on your list that were easy to name? Difficult to name?
>
> Is it possible for you to experience gratitude for the changes in your life? Or do you take them for granted?

Something Is Missing

I decided to treat myself to donuts for breakfast. I don't often do this so when I do it is a special treat.

When we look at a donut it looks just about perfect. And yet on closer examination, if look at a bit differently we notice that something is missing; there is no center. Depending on how we look at it, the donut is either perfect or it is flawed; and yet the fact that it is missing the hole makes it complete and perfect.

It is easy, and we have a lot of practice seeing the flaws in our lives. Sometimes we focus only on what is missing in our lives. Yet when we consider our lives from the perspective of the Lotus Sutra we can begin to see that our lives no matter how seemingly flawed are in fact the perfect life and present the perfect condition for the emergence of our Buddhahood.

Our lives are actually complete from the perspective of the practice of Buddhism. There is nothing missing. While there may be things in our lives that we can change or improve upon we should also consider that each one of those things actually could represent strengths, something we can change into a positive.

It isn't necessary to become someone else; it is only necessary to redirect our lives completely to enlightenment. When we can look at our lives like we look at a donut and realize that the apparent flaws are actually what make us unique and uniquely qualified to attain perfect enlightenment. The donut is perfect for what it is because it is missing the center and has a hole in it.

> What is your default mode of making observations; do you focus on what is missing or what is present?
>
> Looking closely and intensely at one fault, can you find a positive aspect of that fault?
>
> Rather than trying to eliminate the fault how about enhancing the positive?

Problems

It isn't possible to live a life without some problem or obstacle arising. The challenge in our lives is to see the arising of each problem as an opportunity to change something in our lives that caused the problem.

Mistakenly we cling to the notion that we posses complete control of all things connected with our lives. This is a flawed point of view because our body is not an absolute entity. Our body undergoes changes regardless of our intent. We age, we grow sick, and we eventually face death.

If we think about a king who rules his kingdom having the power to praise or punish according to his own will who then becomes ill and faces death. No matter how much power he may have he is powerless to affect his own life in a fundamental way.

Because we seek the power to control things in our lives we fail to seek that which can ultimately give us the ability to end suffering. We seek mistakenly to eliminate suffering by clinging to mistaken views. We may think that if we only had just a little more money or a better house or a better job or a different spouse that all things would be well. We merely look at the surface and think that the conditions that surround us are the things we need to change, never looking at our lives and seeing what we need to change within ourselves.

Seeing that we are fundamentally enlightened beings who are living lives of common people can allow us to see the heart of the cause for suffering and free our minds from the attachments that actually are the root of sufferings.

> Is there any part of sufferings you may experience that are caused by seeking to change things in your environment as opposed to making changes in your own life?
>
> Is your happiness firmly rooted at the core of your life, or dependent on factors in your environment?

Delivery

A while back I had a part-time job delivering pizza. My hours were mostly in the evening since that was the only time I had available to work. In the summer it wasn't so bad making the deliveries at night because it didn't become dark until almost the time I was scheduled to get off. However, in the fall and winter when it got dark early it was very challenging. The problem was folks would order pizza and their houses would either not have house numbers or numbers that were difficult to see from the street, or they would not turn on their house lights.

Our daily service in praise of the Lotus Sutra begins with preparing the altar for service. Then we engage in the practice

of reciting the sutra and chanting the sacred title. It is like we are making sure our house numbers show clearly and our lights are turned on as we invite the protective deities of the universe into our lives.

Without the proper directions, markings, and lights it is difficult for the pizza to be delivered. So too, without opening up our lives, and calling upon the universe using the proper praise it is difficult for the protection to be available. Nichiren himself wrote that because the people of Japan had abandoned the Lotus Sutra, the protective deities had left the nation.

Enjoy your daily practice as you strengthen your faith and your connection with the truth of the Lotus Sutra and thereby live in harmony with the universe.

> When you do your daily service are you mindful of opening up your life to all the positive influences in the universe? Or is it a practice of stating demands and expectations?
>
> What is the focus of your practice, or you life? Is it opportunity or expectations?
>
> What is your mindset, is it your practice should meet your defined expectations, or is it finding value and benefit in the opportunities?

Excitement

As some of you may know I love dogs. There isn't anything wrong with cats; it is just that I have, for most of my life had one or more dogs for pets. I think one of the things that I find I like most about dogs is their genuine excitement over almost any attention you give to them. Another is the fact that they just like being around people for the most part, and especially they give you unconditional love.

Sometimes it is difficult to maintain our enthusiasm for practicing and studying the Lotus Sutra. There are some days when it may be all we can do to just chant Odaimoku three times. There will naturally be days like that, so do not be discouraged. But in our hearts if we can maintain and nourish the kind of eagerness to stay connected with the teachings of the Buddha, then even gradually our lives will undergo a significant change.

One of attitudes toward our practice that Bodhisattvas try to cultivate is childlike. That is with an open-eyed pure eagerness to embrace Buddhism in our lives without all the filters and conditions that we impose upon things as we age. If we think of a puppy or a young child, someone who is eagerly and openly enjoying every experience then we can really begin to get to the depths of having the sutra expounded to ourselves.

> Is your practice childlike, with eagerness and excitement?
>
> Do you greet the start of every day with enthusiasm and excitement?

One Who Does You No Good

We interact with a variety of people all day long as we go through our lives. If we are in school, or work, or even if we hardly go anywhere at all we are interacting with countless people. Some of these interactions are direct, others less so. When someone helps us accomplish something we are usually grateful, especially if we were unable to do it on our own. Sometimes people help us for no reason other than just to be nice, other times it may be because they wish our help in return. We are the same way frequently ourselves. It is easy to help our friends, those people whom we know; it is also perhaps easy to help someone who will be able to return the favor.

How easy though is it for us to help someone or treat someone nicely who can do absolutely nothing of any value for us, someone who is completely incapable of returning the favor, or even who has no idea that you did something for them? How do we treat the person who can do us no good?

There is another action that is difficult to perform as well, and that is having compassion and offering concern even when the other person may not need it. When I think about the difference between the actions of the original disciples of the Buddha who approached the Buddha asking for a prediction of their future enlightenment, and the actions of the Bodhisattvas from beneath the ground who approached the Buddha and only asked about the health of the Buddha I am struck by the contrast. As Bodhisattvas practicing the Lotus Sutra we assume many different personalities, the variety among us is endless. There are also countless others who are not practicing the Lotus Sutra who have many different personalities as well and require our examples to inspire them to practice the Lotus Sutra.

> Do you struggle helping others or being compassionate to those who don't meet certain of your criteria?
>
> Can you easily be compassionate for someone who may not even appreciate your compassion?
>
> Do you live your life with the awareness that when someone praises you they are praising the Buddha within and thereby making causes for their own future enlightenment?

Distorted Buddha

One more than one occasion I have been asked: "Do you worship that fat happy guy?" It is understandable that folks who know nothing about Buddhism would be confused over this image, the image of Hotei who really is not a Buddha at all but is instead a Bodhisattva. It is also understandable that people may think that we pray to the Buddha to perform some miracle or for protection or some other wish fulfilling

function, when in fact we do not. These are understandable and forgivable misunderstandings by folks who do not know our religion and who may genuinely be trying to understand.

These thoughts do however bring up the idea of our own individual distortions of the Buddha and Buddhism as taught in the Lotus Sutra. The Lotus Sutra, being a Mahayana teaching, follows the pattern of greater connection to and relationship with the teachings of the Buddha and the Buddha himself by the practitioners of the teachings. The Mahayana effort was to bring Buddhism back to the common people and to dislodge it from the confines of the monastery. But how willing are we to actually approach Buddhism and Buddha as a possibility in our own lives, as a guaranteed condition of our seemingly ordinary existence?

It is easy, especially when we are in great difficulty, to seek to be rescued by some outside source. It is sometimes very easy to think we do not possess the resources within our own lives, and so are unable to call out the solution from the depths of our existence. When we do that, however, we are actually engaging in a distortion of the Buddha and a distortion of our inherent Buddha potential. It is important to always keep in mind that the fundamental aim of the Buddha in teaching the Lotus Sutra was to reveal not only his eternal nature but also the equality of all beings and the great desire to enable all beings, you and I included, to become Buddhas.

For those of us who practice in a Nichiren denomination we have the representation of the Lotus Sutra and the eternal Buddha depicted on the calligraphic mandala. It is not uncommon for some to view this picture as the actual thing that enables enlightenment. Again this too is a distortion, as the enlightenment is something we already possess and not something that resides outside our lives and which we need to somehow meld with or absorb. We already have it. The picture representation, however it appears, is merely a tool for us to use to awaken to our already existing Buddhahood.

> What distortions of Buddhism do you cling to?
>
> When in times of crisis where do you first seek answers? Within self (subject) or within something outside yourself (object)?

Where Are You

Writing these short meditation essays is an engaging activity causing me to look at things in different ways in order to find connections between our everyday lives and the teachings presented in the Lotus Sutra. I have always looked for Buddhism in everyday experiences but writing it down and sharing has been a new experience. One question that arises is who is reading these things? Another question is where are you when you are reading the posts?

Take a moment right now and look about you and consider where you are. Are you in a comfy spot; are you in your kitchen sipping a cup of coffee or tea? Perhaps you're on some public transportation reading on your way to or from work. You might also be at work, sneaking some me time for yourself. Or perhaps you are in some uncomfortable place; some place that is not a pleasant place to be.

All of those are one way of looking at and responding to the question, where are you. But there is an equally viable alternative way to consider the question and that is where are you personally in your life? Where are you spiritually in your life? Where are you?

It is easy and customary for us to take things at such a rapid pace, living our lives in a mad rush from one destination to another or from one goal to the next. Even if we consider the question from the physical space perspective how many of us have really stopped to take in our physical space, just sitting with it and looking at it with new vision. And especially if we consider the same question from the spiritual or non-physical perspective how frequently do we listen to our own inner voice and ask ourselves where we are?

> Take a moment now and look around you, slowly. What do you see? What would be a detailed description of your environment if you were to describe it to someone not present or even who may not have sight?
>
> Now take some time and look inside your life. How would you describe your life to a friend, a relative, a stranger?

How Long Should I Chant?

Frequently I am asked how long should I chant? Sometimes this question is asked by folks who may have previously been told that they should chant an hour or more a day, or some other fixed goal.

Consider this: you can scrub a floor as a free person or as a slave. It is fundamentally up to you. We all have activities we must engage in, some several times a day, some less frequently. You can cultivate in yourself your own sense of freedom or entrapment.

Chanting the Odaimoku, Namu Myo Ho Ren Ge Kyo, can be much the same way. If we enslave ourselves to the Odaimoku then we are not cultivating happiness for ourselves.

Odaimoku can be chanted at any moment and during any activity we engage in or experience throughout our lives. And when we do this we can engage in a meditative activity regardless of what we are doing. We can meditate as we brush our teeth, or as we sit on the toilet, or as we cook our meals, or scrub the floor. It is simply a matter of what we choose to do and how we choose to do it.

I heard an interesting research project into exercise and burning calories. In test groups those who considered simple things like walking or even sitting as exercise and not just merely a chore, or job, or necessary evil. The folks who thought about exercise value in the activities actually burned more calories than those who did not think of the activity as exercise. The mind is a very powerful organ in our bodies, one we frequently do not use to its maximum.

Of course it is perfectly acceptable and even optimum to set aside a certain amount of time, a dedicated time, to perform our Buddhist practice such as reciting the sutra and chanting. You can set this time aside in the morning upon arising or in the evening before retiring, or you can do both. But in either case if there is no cultivation of joy and appreciation then the results will not be the same as if there is joy and appreciation. We should not become a slave to the action.

Cultivate a mind of joy in all things, chant the sacred title of the Lotus Sutra with great joy and at all times.

> Considering your daily activities, are you able to cultivate joy, awareness, value, and so forth in your attitude while doing those activities?
>
> Do you chant because you want to and because it brings you joy, or do you chant for specified lengths of time expecting joy to occur at completion?

Inner Peace

Numerous people become interested in Buddhism because they are looking for inner peace. Inner peace seems to be the most well known feature or benefit of Buddhist practice. Of course there is much more to Buddhism than inner peace or self-improvement. Regardless though the reason why a person begins to practice Buddhism it all begins by being self aware, aware of one's self.

The beginning of the cultivation of inner peace is actually to look within one's self. Inner peace is not some condition that is induced; it is an innate natural state of being. It begins by recognizing peace in your mind.

If we consider for a moment the things or stuff that happens around us all day long. Things occur, they are neutral but we attach value to them, which is not necessarily bad, it just occurs. But when we can begin to stop the process of rationalizing, of assigning value, or any of the other labels we attach to stuff, then we can just watch the mind and you begin to become part of the whole. There is no longer an outside or inside there is just the experience.

Remember though, we are not letting go just for the sake of letting go. If we cling to the concept of letting go then we are not letting go we are not freeing ourselves, and we will not feel peace. Freeing the mind frees ourselves and then we can act in a less stressful way.

It is how we respond to things as they arise around us that determines our state of mind; it isn't the things themselves. Remember we need to do something; we need to think something in order to become angry or sad or any other emotion.

Chanting the Odaimoku and meditating on the Lotus Sutra enables us to develop a state of mind, which is free from clinging, and one that recognizes that we are already Buddhas, even if we are unaware at the moment.

> Consider trying to avoid attaching values to thing that occur and open yourself up to possibilities possible in all experiences.
>
> Can you recall an instance in your life where attaching a value actually prevented you from joy and benefit?

Witnessing A Great Event

It is simply amazing the things we are able to witness today. The fact that information from almost any place on earth is practically instantly available to us, not just in words but in living color and in motion as well is almost unimaginable when you consider things as they were a mere lifetime ago. We have the ability to see the good and the bad, though most frequently the images provided are of bad.

With the aid of computer generated imagery we are also able to watch scenes in movies that enable us to explore fantasy as if it were reality. There is almost nothing that cannot be done in movies, though I imagine we haven't seen the limit yet.

We are able to walk through doors in the mind through our eyes that previous creators, artists of all kinds, could only dream of and attempt through limited media to recreate.

I have frequently remarked that it would be nice to see a movie version of the stupa that arises from the ground and the emergence of the Bodhisattvas from underground. I think it could be a truly epic production, and certainly would be epic in its message.

But we do not have to wait for some creative person to take on the task. It isn't necessary to depend on someone else to generate the visuals or the music. We can see that play out any day we choose if we awaken to the reality of it in our present lives.

When we chant Odaimoku, Namu Myoho Renge Kyo, we can begin to see our lives, and our environment in new ways. We begin to recreate our own emergence from the dirt of suffering and rise up to bow before the Buddha and greet him. We see our lives as Buddhas and our land as the Buddha's realm. When we see all this then we can show it to others.

> Has your Buddhist practice enabled you to see things about yourself that were previously unobserved?
>
> Have there been questions at the end of some of these essays that have caused you to feel uncomfortable?
>
> Have these questions been questions you have considered previously?

Rainy Day

If I have a choice for weather I would prefer it would rain or snow. I know most people express a preference for sunny weather, I enjoy sunny weather as well, but still I prefer rain. To me rainy weather isn't gloomy; it makes me feel energized and alive. And there is something exciting about snow as well.

As I sit here writing this it is starting to rain and it got me to thinking about how we view things as they occur in our lives. When it's raining how do you feel? Does it cause you to feel sad or blue? What do you see when it rains? Do you view it as something to make life miserable for you?

It is possible for us to look at rain in any number of different ways, just as it is possible to look at our problems in many different ways. Depending upon how we view the problems that arise in our life it will have a significant affect on our life. If we view problems, like rain that depresses up, then we may feel helpless and defeated. On the other hand if we are able to look at our problems in a different light, then we can see them as opportunities to change something in our lives.

It isn't easy sometimes to look at our situation and be thankful or even rejoice, especially when faced with multiple and seemingly complex problems. It isn't easy to always be rejoicing at the appearance of yet one more difficult situation. It is only by taking the test that we can pass. It is only by facing the problem will we be able to change our lives.

Never giving up, always striving, holding firm faith, and steadfast practice assures us all of the great benefit of enlightenment. A practice based firmly on the Lotus Sutra assures us of an enlightenment equal to that of all the Buddhas.

> Recall times of crisis in your past. When you were faced with a crisis what got you through it that time?
>
> The next time you face a crisis make a determination to use the skills you developed in the past.
>
> Chant Odaimoku with a calm meditative mind allowing your inner wisdom to gain its voice.

Release

After spending roughly two years in exile at Izu Peninsula Nichiren was officially pardoned in 1263. The event that precipitated this first of two exiles was Nichiren submitting the Rissho Ankoku Ron, "Treatise On Establishing the Correct Teaching for the Peace of the Land".

When we are released from some thing, which has caused us grief, we feel as if a great burden has been lifted from our lives. It can feel very good to know that we have overcome some hardship. We may even breathe a sigh of relief, or we may celebrate. In any case there comes a degree of happiness when our load is lightened.

Practicing the Lotus Sutra provides a way for us to overcome suffering. Fundamentally we do this by changing in ourselves the causes for suffering. It isn't by some magical process that provides avoidance of difficulties or by waving a wand and making them vanish. By changing our lives, by removing the "dust and dirt of illusions" we are able to firmly establish a foundation upon which gradually we find true happiness.

By chanting Odaimoku, reciting and studying the Lotus Sutra we can achieve release from suffering. As we change our lives we also begin to change our environment. Further as we change those things, we provide examples to our friends and relatives, we show them how it is possible to also become happy.

Again, we do this not by avoiding negative events in our lives, but by facing them head on, by enduring the lesson, so to speak, and learning what causes suffering and what causes happiness. Day by day, we persevere and we strive. It may seem insurmountable in the moment of experience but as we look back we can definitely see changes taking place.

> How easy is it for you to eagerly face an obstacle and say I want to overcome this rather than I wish it hadn't happened or I wish I could avoid this thing?
>
> When you chant do you chant for a specific solution or do you open yourself up to possibilities?

Before You Knew What You Know

"Don't be in a hurry to condemn because he doesn't do what you do or think as you think or as fast. There was a time when you didn't know what you know today." - Malcolm X

It is very easy for us to become critical of people who don't view life the way we do. It is also equally easy for us to look at other people and criticize them for their shortcomings, always quick to be able to identify their faults. We may even be very capable of doing the same to ourselves; never being happy or content and enjoying our lives.

It is difficult sometimes though, for us to celebrate the accomplishments of others. In our very competitive world we may find it difficult to genuinely be happy for the happiness of those we interact with. We may even begrudge our own achievements, finding ways to diminish what we have accomplished or what others have accomplished.

Going lightly on ourselves, realizing that the teaching of the Buddha in the Lotus Sutra are peaceful and pleasant and we can obtain wonderful merits, means that we should abandon wrong views. Being gentle of mind is being gentle towards others and ourselves. Learning to celebrate the good things, to even see the good things in our lives takes practice and skill, especially if we have listened to our mental tapes or the messages of others that try to tell us we are not worthy.

Try this out. Today for half the day look around you and really pay attention to all the things that are red. See if you can spot all the red things in your environment. For the second half try to spot all the green things, look closely and see if you can see green things you never thought of as green before.

Depending upon what we focus our attention to is what we will actually 'see'. Look closely at your life and learn to view the joy you have.

> If you did the red and green exercise were you surprised at how many things you saw?
>
> Did you see things you had overlooked in the past?
>
> In your life what is the first thing you see?
>
> Is it easier for you to focus on the things that are wrong or is it easier to focus on the things that are good?

Do Good

"My country is the world, and my religion is to do good." - Thomas Paine

It is not enough to do no harm; we should seek to do good. Sometimes it can be discouraging to carry this out, especially if we look around and see examples of those who seek only to serve themselves. It is almost as if everyone is out to better only themselves and could care less about others and how they fare.

In Buddhism though, we learn that we should always strive to do good, not only for ourselves but for others as well. Considering not only if we will benefit personally from some act, we try to look into how it will benefit others.

The Buddha taught the Eightfold Path as the way to eliminate suffering. We may wonder how it is we can eliminate suffering merely by following this way. If we look at the word 'right' in each of the eight instructions and we consider it from the perspective of right versus wrong then we will continue to suffer because we will form a perspective of judgment; trying to decide who or what is right and what is wrong.

Instead, when we consider right from the perspective of what is most skillful and what will do the most good or even sometimes what will do the least harm, then we can begin to approach each of these in a different perspective. By trying to always consider what will do the most good, not only for ourselves but for others as well, we not only accumulate merit but we increase the good being done in society.

By changing our behavior and thoughts we can then create new outcomes in our lives, different from the outcomes that cause suffering for ourselves and for others. I think one of the first, though perhaps the most difficult, places to begin is to really strive to see all beings as worthy of respect, even if their actions are not respect worthy.

Even by taking the time to look someone in the eye and say sincerely from the bottom of our hearts that we have gratitude for their efforts, for their presence, we can make a significant impact on the lives of others. Next time you are in the check out line and you come to the cashier, that anonymous person who rings up our purchases, greet them in such a way; plant joy in their lives. Honor them, respect them, cherish them, and praise them, just as Bodhisattva Never-Despise.

> If you already greet the anonymous people in your life you interact with, such as cashiers, try also thanking them for the work they do.
>
> How easy or difficult is it for you to hold your reactions in check when the greeting is not returned?
>
> When you do something good for someone and the effort is not appreciated or acknowledged what are your feelings?

Difficult To See Buddha

"It is difficult to see a Buddha" - Lotus Sutra, Chapter I

Thinking about this phrase I am always struck by the differing ways this can be interpreted. On the one hand the sutra is specifically referring to how rare it is to encounter a Buddha in one's lifetime; the fact that Buddhas only physically appear on rare occasions. Here on this earth we have the historical Buddha who appeared and taught some 2500 years ago. There is also the prediction of the appearance of Maitreya at some point in the distant future, who will teach for a limited amount of time, numbering supposedly just a few days at most.

Another meaning is we fail to perceive the eternally existing Buddha in the universe. It is difficult for us to look at life and see there is the Buddha present in every moment, in every breath. Of course through our practice and study of the Lotus Sutra we know, at least theoretically, that the Buddha is ever present and never disappears.

Another possible interpretation is that within our own lives it is difficult for us to see the Buddha. Also, that it is difficult for us to see the Buddha in other beings. Sometimes this difficulty is because we don't want to see the Buddha either in others or ourselves. We may have ingrained in our minds that we are not worthy or that we are incapable of being such a thing as a Buddha. We may even hold that opinion of others also, thinking that there is no way this or that person, with the way they act, or the way they think, that they could be a Buddha.

In so many ways it is easy for us to actually deny the Buddha, the very thing, which we seek to understand. We think the Buddha isn't here; this place is too messed up. We think the Buddha isn't in me; I'm too messed up. We think the Buddha isn't in others; they're too messed up.

Bodhisattva Never-Despise was able to see the Buddha in others, and the Buddha tells us that he always is here. But this

is difficult to believe, and difficult to practice.

Part of the process of becoming enlightened is, I believe, to develop the ability, to awaken within us the capacity to begin to see our own Buddha potential and then to see it in others. It is to learn to not deny in others or ourselves the very promised reality of being Buddhas. Enlightenment is after all being awakened.

How much are you like the person you most dislike?

If there is someone in your life who gives you grief, or causes you trouble, or makes you feel uncomfortable try looking at the things where the two of you are the most alike, and try looking at all the things in the other person that are actually good and praiseworthy.

If there is no one in your life at the moment who causes you to be upset then do the same for someone with whom you only mildly tolerate, or even those you like. Can you form a deeper sense of appreciation for the many different people in your life?

Do you try to only be in relationship/friendship with people just like you?

Do you chant or practice to change others or do you seek to change yourself?

The Ninety Nines

"Courage is the price life extracts for granting peace." - Amelia Earhart

Amelia Earhart, born in 1897, is probably the most famous woman pilot. During her forty-year life she distinguished herself as an aviation pioneer and author. She received many awards and accomplished many firsts. The Ninety Nines was a organization she helped to found for the purpose of supporting other women pilots.

Courage is not an obscure word yet I would like to share a definition here; mental or moral strength to venture, persevere, and withstand danger, fear, or difficulty. - Webster Dictionary

I am not sure how you feel after reading that or what it brings to your mind, but to me it describes very accurately how we practice the Lotus Sutra; we practice with courage. Daily we challenge both our mental and moral strength to carry out a very difficult practice, sometimes in environments that are less than supportive. Practicing the Lotus Sutra requires of us to persevere even in the face of sometimes seemingly insurmountable obstacles.

The Buddha, in a previous life as Never-Despising Bodhisattva is frequently used as an inspiration for how we honor the lives of all beings, bowing to the Buddha in each life. Yet, this Bodhisattva also is an inspiration for the courage to practice in less than ideal circumstances.

> Have you ever considered your Buddhist practice as courageous?
>
> The Buddha is called the Hero of the World, is that a title you could also claim for yourself?

Great Wave

There was a famous artist in Japanese history who is most well known because of a famous woodblock print he did of a giant wave. Katsushika Hokusai, when in his 60's and 70's, created a series of woodblocks depicting various views of Mount Fuji. One of his most famous, if not the most famous was an image of a large wave rising out of the ocean and curling downward on some small boats.

The wave is by some thought to be a tsunami wave, but in fact it is an okinami, or literally a large wave of the open sea. In this picture there are three boats.

I don't want to attribute meanings to the picture that I am not sure the artist intended, but I can't help but be reminded of the image of oceans and boats frequently used in Buddhism.

The Dharma is the boat, which can withstand the tidal forces as we navigate our passage from one shore to the other.

There are many people suffering in this world today, perhaps you are one of those who feel as if you are being tossed around. Perhaps you may feel as if there are so many troubles that you are drowning in an ocean of suffering.

There is a story told of Nichiren on his way to his second exile; his trip to Sado Island. It is said that the water was so rough that all those on board the boat feared for their lives. According to the story, Nichiren took one of the oars and with the blade wrote the Odaimoku onto the surface of the water in order to calm the sea.

Whether or not you believe this happened exactly as it is told, there is certain documentary support for believing that he actually did attempt to do this. Still the fact of the matter is that Nichiren placed all of his faith in the power of the Lotus Sutra. We too can cast the Odaimoku upon the ocean of our suffering, and with our practice we can calm the waters. We can change ourselves so that we can safely and confidently navigate the rough seas in which we may find ourselves.

> When chanting Odaimoku how easy is it for you to chant to calm your mind versus chanting to solve a problem?
>
> Which do you do first; seek calming of self or solutions to events outside?

Tuning In

When I was growing up my first radio was a quartz radio that I built. I ran a wire out of my bedroom window and attached it to the outside water faucet, which served as the antenna. There wasn't much you could get on a quartz radio, but it did offer some 'magical' entertainment. Now a day's iPods are the magical entertainment.

During my childhood, there was no such thing as a portable radio. It wasn't until around the time when I entered Junior High School, or Middle School now, that I got my first transistor radio, which offered musical portability. The music was not stereo but at that time who cared. It was so neat having this big portable box to carry around so you could listen to radio, AM at that.

Of course at that time who would have imagined that we could stream music from anywhere in the world while walking around our neighborhood; heck we don't even need to be connected to the internet by a home computer anymore. We can tune in to almost anything we want to listen to!

And that's the truth, you can tune it to whatever you want, or tune out what you don't want. When it comes to your personal inner radio station, I wonder what you tune in to. Do you tune into messages of failure, or tapes playing inside your head saying you can't do something, or you're not worthy? Do you have a station preset to uncertainty, or doubt?

How easy is it for you to find the Buddha's station? Let's all sing songs of great praise and joy as we calmly overcome our troubles.

> Which station do you tune in to first when you face some difficulty?
>
> What music does that station play; sounds of silence, or tunes of trepidation, or drums of doubt?
>
> Do you tune in to the Odiamoku of your life?

Winding Path

Not too long ago I was touring one of the Revolutionary War era battlefields that is located near Charlotte. It was interesting walking along the paths and reading the different placards with information about what occurred at each particular location.

I was struck by how straight and direct the paths were. All the paths were paved, and though they wound around through the area, they basically were fairly direct and easy to walk. Yet we know that it wasn't the case for the participants in the battle.

They had to deal with undergrowth, thorns, and brambles; all sorts of things prohibited their easy maneuvering through the area. Yet now all that was cleared away making for a nice easy stroll with my puppy.

Our journey along the path of enlightenment is much the same; at least that's what I think. We look at our path in front of us and we see all manner of obstacles, we see lots of things to hinder our progress. Yet when we look back on what we have accomplished we may not see them. We may also look at other folks, and think they have an easy time navigating their journey.

It is easy to focus our attention on the immediate challenges we face and easy to loose sight of the goal of our practice. We may sometimes fail to consider that a different road, one with fewer troubles, would not provide us the fertile ground upon which to accomplish the changes we need to make in our own lives.

The way to transform our lives is not by avoiding our tribulations but by going through them and making them the cause for our enlightenment.

With confidence that we can overcome all of our obstacles through the power of faith in the Lotus Sutra, through the power of our upholding the Odaimoku, we can purify our world and travel over clear paths lined with golden ropes and jeweled trees. All of these we create through our practice.

The mind has a remarkable capacity for forgetting pain even while remembering the pain event. Have you had experiences in your life when looked back on you wonder why you were so concerned or what the big deal was?

With each life event we have an opportunity to learn new life skills. Thinking of the problems, no matter how small, you face at the moment, what life skills do you think you will learn in the process?

Do you think about difficulties as opportunities to learn something new in your life?

History

I have had the wonderful opportunity to be able to travel to Japan and England on several occasions. The thing that impresses me the most about my travels is the sense of history. In England there are buildings, which are older than the country of the United States. You walk around London and you are surrounded by a history that makes the US seem like an infant. The same is true in Japan, though in truth many of the old buildings there are in fact reconstructions of old buildings that have been destroyed. In Japan the sense of history is much more fluid than in England, at least that is my impression.

In England the history is solid, manifest in the old structures that are everywhere. In Japan the history is more of a concept of a connection to the past not dependent upon a permanently existing structure.

I once visited Wupatki, a prehistoric Native American structure that dates back over 800 years ago, so there is ancient history in America as well. But at this pueblo there has not been continuous habitation.

Our historical connection with the past can manifest in any number of different ways. There can be the physical presence of something concrete; on one hand still being used and on the other not being used. There is also a sense of history that is more of a connection to the past through less concrete structures.

In the Lotus Sutra, we have a distant connection to the past as well as the infinite future. In this instance the connection and the history depends upon our actions in the present to manifest the reality of the historical event. The Lotus Sutra depends not on the actual physical presence of some thing that existed before us, but on the connection we create with the past and the future.

Because of the ray of light the Buddha emitted those present in the congregation were able to see far into the past; they were able to see Buddhas, and stupas of those Buddhas. In various places in the Lotus Sutra, the Buddha reveals the past causes of a variety of people so they can know the causes made which enabled them to become Buddhas.

We may think that these are not things we can accomplish. Yet through our daily practice of the Odaimoku and faith in the Lotus Sutra, we are able to reveal the historical truth of the Bodhisattvas who arose from beneath the earth. We can, by chanting Odaimoku manifest the life of these great Bodhisattvas and reveal our infinite connection with the Eternal Buddha.

> When you practice do you do so with a sense of connection to the eternal?
>
> Is the story of the Lotus Sutra real in your life today?
>
> How can you make the Lotus Sutra more alive and relevant in your life?

Concern For Others

The numbers are sobering. Every year some 15 million people die of hunger. Do we even know what 15 million is, can we comprehend that number? New York city has a population of 8.3 million, and Los Angeles is 9.8 million. So if we eliminated the entire population of Los Angeles and half the population of New York city every year that would be a fair representation of the number of people who die from hunger in one year. Now do that every year. It is frightful.

This doesn't even address the number of children who die as infants, the number of homeless, and so on. We just aren't doing a very good job of taking care of each other. In the United States, we live in relative comfort for the most part. We consume as if there is no end to resources and completely oblivious to the suffering taking place all over the globe. Life goes on.

You know I have written a lot about our personal practice, our practice to attain enlightenment. We cannot understand enlightenment without considering the suffering of others. We will not truly become happy until we enable all other to do so as well. The first of the Bodhisattva vows speaks of enabling all living beings to become enlightened, even before we do so.

"I offered him anything he wanted. I collected fruits, drew water, gathered firewood, and prepared meals for him. I even allowed my body to be his seat. I never felt tired in body and mind. I served him for a thousand years. In order to hear the Dharma from him, I served him so strenuously that I did not cause him to be short of anything." (Lotus Sutra, Chapter XII)

This passage, from the Devadatta Chapter tells how the Buddha served Devadatta in a previous life so that he could be taught the Wonderful Dharma of the Lotus Flower Sutra. When I think about the truth of the Buddha being present in all beings as taught by Never-Despising Bodhisattva I can't help but think that we can begin to really understand the teaching of the Lotus Sutra when we serve other beings, when we can help them as the Buddha did seeking the Dharma from Devadatta.

I encourage you to strive to find ways, even small ones, to give of yourself to ease the sufferings of others. Practice compassion.

> What are some possible ways in which you can alleviate the sufferings of others?
>
> Have you considered creating gift bags filled with personal hygiene items, first aid items, perhaps a protein bar, putting it all into zip lock bags and keeping them in your car to hand to those who you see begging on street corners. Or how about passing out emergency Mylar blankets?
>
> What are some other creative ways you could do some small good?

Vision

For those of you who know me know that I wear glasses. I have worn glasses since I was in my teens, though occasionally I did use contact lenses. As I have gotten older my vision has deteriorated to the point now where I need trifocal lenses. Without these glasses I would be seriously limited in what I would be able to do. My life would be drastically different. For one thing I wouldn't be able to drive, nor would I be able to read, something I really enjoy doing.

In many ways, even if we have perfect or near perfect eyesight, we all need corrective lenses. Our Buddhist practice helps us to create the correct lens through which to see the reality of life, the true nature of cause and effect.

If we look through distorted lenses, not seeing the suffering caused by our unskillful actions we will continue to manifest results we may not wish to experience. Buddhism helps us abandon the distortions that bring on suffering. By following the Eightfold Path we can begin to see how our distorted views cause suffering for ourselves and for others.

Until we remove our ignorance of the cause of suffering and attachments to these causes we won't be able to manifest enlightenment in our lives. We need the corrective lens of the teachings and practice of Buddhism in order to see clearly the causes of our suffering and hindrances to our enlightenment. Chanting the sacred title, Odaimoku, gives us the courage and strength to follow the Eightfold Path and remove the delusions.

> What are the distortions you see? Can you name one or two?
>
> What might you do to change your views?

Legos

It could be Legos or it could be anything. How many times have you gotten some item that required some assembly and just jumped right in without reading the instructions?

Children are frequently enthralled with the bright colored building blocks that snap together and can be used to construct all manner of things. Legos can be used to build almost anything the imagination can conceive. But sometimes our ability to conceive something is limited by our ability to assemble the pieces. That is why directions can be very helpful.

I know that I consider myself to be a somewhat clever person, sometimes too clever for my own good. I have on numerous occasions taken out of the box some item I have purchased that requires assembly, and jumped right in putting things together. Yet often times I find that I have to take something back apart because I didn't realize that I had done things out of order. Other times I realize that I can't quite get it to work just right. I pull out the instructions and either undo what I have already done or begin again.

We are given the perfect instructions in the Lotus Sutra for our individual attainment of enlightenment. It really doesn't matter who we are, or even who we think we are, we can achieve the same enlightenment as all the Buddhas, though it will be unique to our individual selves.

The directions are pretty straightforward, they are not complex, though they are difficult to maintain. Keeping, or upholding the sutra, reading it, reciting it, copying it and teaching are all we have to do. Praising the Lotus Sutra in all we do is fundamentally at the heart of each of these things.

It isn't the body of the Buddha we praise it is the teachings, which are perfectly contained within the Lotus Sutra.

> Do you take shortcuts in your Buddhist practice? Honestly?
>
> Do you view your entire day's activities as Buddhist practice or do you set boundaries; some things Buddhist and other things not?
>
> What is the first thing you do when you wake up? Is it to chant the Odaimoku?

Chiaroscuro

Chiaroscuro is an Italian word that means "light-dark". I first ran across this word when I was studying fine art way back, a long time ago. In art it is the contrast between light and dark, or the tonal values of a painting, though it also has other meanings in various art forms. Generally though it is about contrasts.

One way to observe a painting is to study the tonal qualities of the artwork, and frequently the stark contrasts between light and dark can say more to the viewer than the colors in the painting. In fact if a very colorful painting has no tonal contrasts, that is there is no light and dark, then the painting will be very bland and not so pleasing to the eye.

Our lives are much the same way. If it weren't for the variations in our personalities, our tendencies and so forth we would all be boringly identical. Our lives would also be very ordinary, even if it was all bad or all good, it would still lack contrast and so would be bland.

I read something the other day that said it isn't the big things that really make us happy or unhappy, it is little things. Think about this. The research found that for example on our jobs we gain a sense of happiness or dissatisfaction more from the accumulation of little events throughout the day or days, than we do from one or two major events.

We have a sense of our general disposition more from viewing a series of events than from one event.

Today we are able to practice Buddhism and the Lotus Sutra because we have created the causes to do so.

And by the same method, the accumulation of the merits of our practice we can manifest the Buddha potential within our lives.

Because we have problems we seek out a solution, that

solution is to practice this Lotus Sutra. We will continue to experience difficulties, but we can create great merit for others and ourselves. Thereby we can create a beautiful life full of all the tones and values causing others to praise the sutra.

> How good are you at looking at the small things in your life and finding joy and happiness in them?
>
> Today, as you go through your day try expressing gratitude for everything you encounter. You don't need to say it out loud, merely take a moment and say thank you in your mind.
>
> At the end of the day think about whether or not this was difficult, or easy. Were you able to keep it in your mind all day?

Don't Speak The Language

Have you ever gone some place and didn't speak the language. I remember my first trip to Japan when I wasn't with a group. At that time I also didn't speak any Japanese other than a few standard greetings. It was a stressful trip, though not a bad experience.

The good thing about Japan is that there are usually a lot of signs that are in English, and the bullet train makes stop announcements in English, so that really helps. Yet it isn't easy and carefree if you don't speak any Japanese. For me it was a bit nerve racking and there were lots of anxiety producing moments.

I think one of the neat things about Buddhism is that while it can be confusing at times, there are usually many ways of understanding or explaining the teachings. But ultimately it is through our practice and faith that we can most deeply understand the teachings of the Lotus Sutra.

Just as it is possible to travel to a strange country not speaking the language and have a good time, see a variety of things, and have wonderful experiences, it isn't necessary to have a scholar's understanding of the Lotus Sutra. We do not need to master theory, though we should try to understand the basics, where we need to excel is in our practice and faith.

> Think about your practice, have you gained a greater understanding of life and Buddhism?
>
> Frequently though, sometimes the more we know the less we really understand. Have you experienced this in your practice?
>
> Do you think your practice has leveled off? Grown? Lessened?

Long Flight

When I was younger I used to live in Hawaii. I lived there a total of about 10 years. I really enjoyed living in Hawaii. Every day I could go to the beach and swim in the Pacific Ocean, it is truly a paradise.

There was a period of about six months when I would fly once a month to San Francisco from Honolulu and back. Flying back then was nothing like flying now, not all of it good though; for example smoking was allowed on flights at that time and the planes could get pretty smoky. Also the flights were longer, since planes didn't go as fast as they do now.

On the flight from Honolulu they always played this game where you could guess the time when the flight would reach its halfway point. The pilot would give you the cruise speed, the distance and so forth and then you would submit your answer. The winner would get some small prize and a brief moment of fame as their name would be announced. Also the snack cart would be a volcano with dry ice smoke coming from its mouth. They would serve a punch drink dipped right out of the volcano. It was all very festive.

Keep in mind that the practice of the Lotus Sutra is a lifetime endeavor is difficult. Unlike hopping on a plane and knowing that the destination is just a matter of hours away, our journey on the Buddhist path is a lifetime endeavor if we are to reach our destination. Along the way we of course have obstacles, turbulence you might say; yet there are truly some victories as well. We can approach our practice as being good regardless of our immediate circumstance, because we know we are changing our lives; something that isn't easy to accomplish.

It is not easy, this is true. We don't realize how much effort we have put into becoming what we are now, or we may not realize how little effort we have put into being who we are. So when we undertake a practice that works on fixing our mistaken views, or tackles our habits, we think it extremely difficult.

We boarded a plane to take us to a destination, enlightenment. The Buddha is our pilot, our fellow Sangha members are also passengers along with us. Together we can reach our goal. Let us together enjoy the good things and recognize the struggles, always making efforts to become enlightened and enable others to do the same.

> Have you ever become discouraged over the pace of change in your life?
>
> If that has happened, did you think about how long it took you to become who you are? Change does not happen over night but it can happen.

Sucked In

"One of the interesting things about success is that we think we know what it means. A lot of the time our ideas about what it would mean to live successfully are not our own. They're sucked in from other people." - Alain de Botton

In the course of our days and lives we have many opportunities to gather information about many things. We learn from our parents about good manners, how to act in socially acceptable ways. We learn many things in the schools we attend. Later on in life as we mature our brain begins a process of sorting out many of the things we have taken on, and sometimes we discard things we deem to be unnecessary.

I wonder though if once we leave adolescence we are always as rigorous about examining the beliefs we have about life. As we enter the work force, however we define that, we learn new rules and sometimes I suspect that we are not as critical of those rules as we once were. We adopt many standards for evaluating our life that are based upon what others view as acceptable. We listen to and take on many values that sometimes are harmful to our general well being.

Are you happy and peaceful? Do we even know what to do to establish a happy and peaceful life? Whose message are we listening to as we go through our lives?

If we knew that the path of our lives was secure, that there was certainty of enlightenment how free would we feel? Would our burdens be easier if we did not have to worry about happiness?

Contained within the Lotus Sutra is the heart and soul of all the messages of all the Buddhas. It isn't easy to believe this; we may struggle with accepting the truth of the message of the Buddha. Yet I wonder how is it easier to accept messages that deny us our ability to be happy. Which message do you allow to penetrate the core of your life?

> Take some time and go back over the several questions proposed in this essay?
>
> Are there truths there for you discover?

Slow And Deliberate

"They proceed to the enlightenment of the Buddha" - Lotus Sutra, Chapter I

Are you late? Have you something to do right now? How's your plan going? Did you check your 'to do' list?

Gosh we are busy people aren't we? Busy people are happy people, right? Never a dull moment. Productivity...that's what's important.

If it's so good, then why do we have to keep trying to convince ourselves how good it is by catchy slogans and pep talks? I mean if it really felt good to be rushed then wouldn't we just know it. Yet there is something in myself that is suspicious about this.

Do I really enjoy my food more just because I have been doing something else while eating, or because I ate it in the car, or finished in a hurry? I know there are times when it may be necessary to be in a hurry, but do we have the ability or even the skill to slow down when we don't need to rush?

When I was much younger I was told about a supposedly Japanese expression that amounted to chew your food 20 times and your face becomes happy. I know when I first tried it all that seemed to happen was my jaw got tired. It is interesting though that if we slow down and focus on what we are doing, we can appreciate it much more.

Sometimes when I am busy doing something, my dog will bring her ball to me for play. I swear she can tell if I am absently tossing the ball or if I am really paying attention, I think she gets her cues from my eyes. I suspect children are the same way, they can tell when we are giving them our undivided attention.

The little things can really be important, and though we may try to kid ourselves into thinking otherwise it really does have an effect in one way or another.

I think our practice of Buddhism is the same. When we really take the time to engage our whole life into our practice, a quality practice we truly benefit more than if we approach our practice from a point of accumulating quantity. This also has a 'spill-over' affect into all areas of our life. Give it a try, go slow and deliberately.

> Before you move on to another essay, spend some time doing things slowly and deliberately?
>
> How difficult is it for you to slow down and be mindfully present in the moment?
>
> Are you an adrenalin junky? Do you feel as though you are not really 'alive' unless you are rushing around?

Self Control

In another essay I invited you to spend half your day observing all the red things you could find, really focusing on red colors. Then I invited you to spend the second half of the day observing all green colored things. This was an attempt to demonstrate that what you focus on influences your life.

Now I want to share with you something interesting I just read. Recent research reported by the Association for Psychological Science "Practicing Self-Control Can Help" discusses the technique for building self-control and the effects of diminished self-control. The study indicated that it is possible for a person to deplete their personal 'self-control' savings bank. When that happens a person is more likely to act in aggressive or at least more stressful ways.

According to this research by simply performing safe acts with the non-dominant hand for extended lengths of time it was possible for a person to increase their self-control. The research showed that doing this really hard for a short term has a somewhat negative impact but if the activity is carried out over an extended time period it actually did improve the reduction of aggressive responses. So it might be hard at first but like exercising it becomes easier over time.

This got me to thinking about our Buddhist practice, which is fundamentally about changing ourselves, and becoming enlightened. Practicing for the long haul yields the greatest benefit.

Sometimes our practice is easy, sometimes it is much harder. Either way our focus should remain on our objective. It seems this is pretty universal advice. Weather it be exercise, which I am sure you know requires constant effort to stay in shape, or now with this research self-control, or Buddhism, the long continued effort is what really yields the greatest results.

I found 20 instances where the Buddha is given the title and honorific, "Controller of Men". Fundamentally this control begins with self.

> Have you considered brushing your teeth with your non-dominant hand? Standing on one foot? All of which are actually very beneficial for you, science has shown.
>
> Have you ever considered facing the opposite direction when you do your sutra recitation? Are you dependent upon facing only the altar?
>
> Sometimes a little change up is good, why not try a candlelight only service at night?

Reorient Your Life

Every day we are constantly being pulled in many directions. I read an article about someone who did a count of the number of times he was notified by his various computer programs, smart phone applications, email and so forth; on average it was one every 6 minutes or 10 times an hour. I can honestly say that my devices aren't as active as that, but I am frequently distracted by various other things

It is easy to loose our direction or to take a detour; an unexpected, unplanned, and sometimes unwanted diversion from our main objective. In some cases the need for the change cannot be avoided, at other times it may be beneficial. I wonder though if we loose the ability to discern when we are being led in directions we really don't want to go and are actually detrimental towards our progress to a goal.

In Buddhism it is easy to be distracted by many things. Life can throw at us so many obstacles that sometimes it is like driving through a heavy rain on a highway and the windshield wipers are going so fast yet we can't see much of the road ahead and so we slow down or pull over.

It isn't easy though in our daily lives to actually slow down, life seems to march inexorably forward with or without us.

At times like these we may feel as if we are passengers on a bus being driven madly forward to a destination not of our choosing.

There are things we can do though once we become aware of this condition. It is possible to limit the number of interrupting distractions. The first thing that helps is to firmly establish the routine of placing our practice first and foremost in our daily lives. When we can begin our day with even the smallest amount of mindful Buddhist practice we set the stage for how we manage our entire lives.

When I was much younger and in the Marine Corps, I was struggling with keeping my practice routine consistent amongst the demands of my daily responsibilities. I went to ask guidance about this and I was told that when I could put my practice first, when I created the time for it, giving it the true importance I felt on an intellectual level it should have. In other words when I actually began to practice in a manner consistent with my mind, that all the other things would in turn find their own place.

When I could reverse the way I approached the problem the change could occur, and the change did occur. Instead of making my Buddhist practice among the many things going on in my life I reoriented things so that Buddhism came before all else. When I did this I found I really had the time to practice and the other things naturally came much easier.

> Try putting your Buddhist practice first before all the other things you need to accomplish.
>
> What were your results?
>
> Did your practice take on more significance in your life?

Stay In Your Own Lane

How often have you driven on the road and had someone creep over into your lane of traffic, or had an on coming car think they needed some space on your side of the highway? I won't say the drivers here are worse than yours, but I do experience it frequently. Or perhaps it has happened that you have veered a little too far over and felt the bump-bump-bump of the pavement warning devices on the side of the road just at the edge of the shoulder.

We obviously understand the dangers of not driving in our own designated space on the road; it can be harmful or even deadly. Yet I wonder if we have the same caution about how we live our lives. Do we find it easy to live outside of our lives, do we let our lives creep into the lives of others?

Every time we make a comparison between our life and the life of someone else we are actually to some degree living someone else's life, we are creeping out of our life into theirs. Straying into someone else's life and out of ours may seem innocuous, relatively harmless, yet it can be very damaging to our own life and potentially deadly to our relationship with others as well. Even if we don't see the effect as dramatically as we would with an auto accident the damage is done none-the-less.

Judging our lives by the standards of another or vice versa does us no good, because there isn't an exact equality of capabilities, living conditions, past causes, social context, family background...and on and on the list could go.

It is interesting that the Buddha didn't say that everyone will be just like he was, or that our lives would be identical. They won't, it isn't possible. But we can actually attain an enlightenment that is equal to the Buddha's, even as it manifests differently in our own unique circumstances.

The same can be said when we compare our life to that of another person. What looks admirable on someone else may not be suitable for our own circumstances.

Our goal is to become enlightened as we are in this life. What is necessary is to find out what within our own life needs to fundamentally change in order to manifest enlightenment. The answer to that search is found only with in us and not in the life of another. It is the changes we make in ourselves that will bring forth enlightenment.

There were those among the Buddha's disciples who upon first hearing the Lotus Sutra, compared themselves to others not realizing that the apparent differences they perceived were really only differences in their own minds and attachments. Let us drive in our own lane, and live our own life.

> Do you find yourself making comparisons between yourself and others?
>
> Are there qualities in others you wished you had, are you sure you don't have your own version of that quality already? Would that quality actually fit you?
>
> Whose life do you live, your own or someone else's?

Is Your Future Another Image Of Your Past?

It is easy for Buddhists to speak of and use the word Karma, frequently almost as if what will happen to us is fixed and impossible to change. Sometimes it can become a default fallback position on which we view the events of the present and the impression of the future.

Sometimes we might find ourselves in the midst of a serious crisis and think to ourselves that it will never get better or that things will never change. I am not sure it is possible for most of us to avoid feeling this way at one time or another in our life.

But consider, if you will, for a moment that all of these setbacks, obstacles, troubles, what ever, are nothing more than stepping-stones along the path of your life.

There is no reason why your life should be limited by your current condition, unless that is what you want. Stopping on the stone you are currently on, though does not get you down the road to happiness.

If you think where you are is dark and isolated remember that this is also the condition from which butterflies emerge.

With our practice of Buddhism it is possible for us to change any karma. We can begin to respond to the things that arise in our life in different ways and thereby experience new outcomes. It isn't necessary for us to remain trapped in a cycle of suffering or despair.

Our future can look entirely different than our past. With the Lotus Sutra, and our Buddhist practice we can even illuminate the sufferings we are experiencing as well as those we have experienced and with the wisdom learned we can forge a future with different outcomes. No matter how dark or how long darkness has existed in our lives, just as a light illuminates a cave that has been dark for hundreds of years, the Lotus Sutra can bring light and enlightenment to our lives.

Do you think of karma as what will happen or what is happening? Actually karma is what you are doing about what you experience; karma is action.

When a crisis or problem or roadblock occurs area you aware of what your default strategy is?

How locked in to your image of your past are you? Do you think about your future only in relation to the past? Or can you imagine a future completely different? How vivid can you make this image?

Umbrella

Umbrellas are pretty handy devices. If we use an umbrella when it is raining we can stay dry, and if we use it during sunny weather we can stay cooler and not burn from the sun. All of those are beneficial uses.

I saw a cartoon the other day, which illustrated a completely different use of an umbrella, and not necessarily for the good. In the picture a man is holding an umbrella open above his body and from the sky lots of little red hearts were 'raining' down. In the illustration the man was completely protected from all these little hearts, and he looked pretty sad.

Do you have an umbrella open above your life that prevents or hinders love and appreciation and lots of good things from falling on you? How open are you to receiving all the good things in life? How open are you to receive the sweet rain of dharma? Do you shade yourself from the light of enlightenment?

Practicing Buddhism is a lot about opening ourselves up. We open our lives up to self-exploration and discovery. Through this process we weed out those things that prevent us from manifesting our inherent Buddha condition. We nourish the process through our practice of chanting the sutra and the Odaimoku, Namu Myoho Renge Kyo. But when we have doubts and when we are not fearless in our efforts, we are protecting that which is in us that causes us suffering, we are keeping an umbrella open that prevents us from becoming happy.

One of my favorite sentences from the Lotus Sutra says, "when you have great joy you will become a Buddha" – Chapter II. I have said it before, however, I think it is worth saying again. When you have great joy, when you allow the joy of the dharma to fill your life then you will become a Buddha. This great joy, I do not believe is the complete elimination of problems but it is the belief in the assurance of being a Buddha.

> How easy or difficult is it for you to receive praise, affection, appreciation, gratitude? Or do you find it easier to give those things than to receive them?
>
> Have you ever given thought to the ways in which you protect yourself from nourishing things in your life, such as the things mentioned above?
>
> Are there things you can do from today that will open yourself up to receiving good things from others?

Setting Your Intention

"Let your intentions be good - embodied in good thoughts, cheerful words, and unselfish deeds - and the world will be to you a bright and happy place in which to work and play and serve" - Grenville Kleiser, American author 1868-1953

When we first set out on our practice of Buddhism generally we have an intention to attain enlightenment. Sometimes some people have that thought even though they may not even know what enlightenment is. Still some people start practicing Buddhism not really sure of what they seek. There are truly a variety of reasons for starting to practice Buddhism.

As we practice and study more, if we didn't already have the intent to become enlightened, we may soon find ourselves wishing to attain what the Buddha experienced. Yet even still, for some the intention of enlightenment isn't nearly as clear as the intention to eliminate suffering or overcome some difficult problem.

Over time though as we continue to practice, or when we overcome our problem, or even when overcoming our difficulty takes longer than we expected, we loose focus. We may become distracted or discouraged because things are harder than we originally thought they would be. It is, I believe, as easy to be discouraged, as it is to be lulled into a sense of complacency.

If we can develop these ways of intention in our lives then we too can become the king of our Sumeru-world with unhindered powers and virtues.

How do we go about doing this? How do we rejuvenate our practice? How do we refocus or even deepen our practice?

Making the Lotus Sutra the core of our life, the center point, the point from which all else radiates is key. Our intention should rest on the Lotus Sutra.

I challenge you, from this day to set your intention to practice the Lotus Sutra deeply, intentionally, and centrally. In the morning just after you open your eyes, even before you get out of bed, say to yourself three Odaimoku, three Namu Myoho Renge Kyo. Say it with gratitude and generosity. Then after you are dressed make time, even a few minutes if that is all you can, and sit down and chant Odaimoku, set your intention to be mindful through the day and live your day based on the Lotus Sutra. Also express appreciation to yourself for how you have begun your day. Finally at the end of the day right before you go to sleep, even as you are laying in bed chant Odaimoku again three times, with your mind on the desire for happiness for all beings and appreciation for your day based on the Lotus Sutra.

Of course, hopefully your day will also include some more time for chanting and reciting the Lotus Sutra. No matter though, at least try doing this, for it is the cause for your happiness and enlightenment.

> Make a serious determination to practice intentionally from arising to retiring. Maybe make a little check list for review at the end of each day. Try to make this a regular activity. Remember it may take 15 or more days before it really settles into a reliable routine way of living.

Three Hindrances To Your Practice

Looking into our lives to find those things that prevent us from accomplishing what we wish is fundamental to Buddhist practice. It isn't always easy to spot them, however. Here is a short list of things you can look for, find out if they are what hinder you.

One common hindrance is to worry obsessively over whether or not we are practicing correctly. By this tight clinging to a need to always get it right or to be perfect we can cause undue stress. Preventing ourselves from experiencing the pure joy of practice hinders our practice.

Instead of worrying about whether you are practicing correctly learn to observe what is going on when you do practice. Be generous with yourself. Look for the mystery. Open up to wonder, as if you were a child again.

Another hindrance is to worry more about time spent practicing than the quality of the practice. In a single moment exists the potential to praise and rejoice, thereby assuring enlightenment. The sole factor is mind at that moment. Let go of attachment to quantity of Odaimoku and embrace quality.

Learn by listening to your life. Open yourself up and become aware of the joy of chanting Odaimoku without concern for length of time. This isn't a job with a time clock only getting paid for time spent.

Also a hindrance is the desire to seek out some new and improved practice. Focus less on the tool and more on the skill. We can become like junk collectors accumulating lots of needless and useless things in an attic. We have the gem; the wisdom to see it and use it is what's important.

> Are you a victim of any of these hindrances?
>
> If you are not then you might consider the hindrance of perfection. We all have something that holds us back.
>
> Thinking again about in a single moment exists the potential to joy or suffering depending upon the condition of the mind. What are your feelings about this?
>
> Focus on feelings not thoughts or intellectual concepts.

Priorities

We all lead very busy lives. Some of us lead hyper-busy lives and some lead ultra-hyper-busy lives. Time is a precious commodity for many of us. Often the reason we say something doesn't get done is because we didn't have time for it.

Language and the words we use are very interesting. Sometimes we can change a word and while the result is the same there is a shift of awareness of the problem in a different way.

Take the example of not having enough time to do something, perhaps your daily practice. Now instead of saying I don't have enough time, try inserting 'it's not a priority'. Hmmm?

I think we almost always manage to get things done that are important to us, especially if we phrase it in such stark language. When we say we don't have time, it is important to ask ourselves if we are just being polite or if we are hiding behind some other reason.

We have only so much time in every day, it truly is a precious commodity. How we use it is critical, and this shift in our language may help to highlight what is important and what isn't. It may allow us to actually get to the bottom of something that is prohibiting us from becoming happy.

> Do you really not have enough time or is it not really important?
>
> Have you previously considered the power of language?
>
> Are there other areas of your life where your words are masking a deeper problem?

Be Better Not Perfect

When looking at the trajectory of our life or our progress in practice it isn't always easy to have a long view. Having a long view makes it possible to see that things over time actually do improve. Progress more often than not is the accumulation of a series of small incremental achievements sometimes accompanied by setbacks.

Embracing the idea of being better and letting go of the need for perfection is one of many keys to becoming happier in our lives. In being better not perfect, the idea is that by

continually making changes, by continually making progress, we actually improve our lives in a much more significant and profound way than if we focused on trying to achieve perfection. Achieving perfection is not possible no matter what and so we are bound to suffer. Desiring perfection is an attachment to something that is impossible to achieve.

"What you are now practicing is the way of Bodhisattvas. Study and practice it continuously, and you will become Buddhas." - Lotus Sutra, Chapter III

Our daily efforts may seem small but over time they accumulate into a significant effort. What may seem quite impossible if we look at the whole actually becomes very doable with continuous effort. The trick is to not be discouraged.

While enlightenment exists in every single moment, it is the accumulation of many moments of practice and effort that enables us to build a solid life full of happiness and joy. It may be impossible to imagine this today, but looking back over your life of accumulated effort you will definitely see significant change.

> Consider doing this gratitude exercise. At the end of every day make a list of all the things you are grateful for. At the end of a week review your list. This need not take more than 5 minutes each day. The objective is to become more aware of what is good in your life. Research has shown that doing this improves outlook and increases positive feelings about one's life.

Delight In The Dharma

Have you ever noticed that when you really like something, when you really enjoy something it is easy to do that thing?

Last night I was on my way home from visiting a member of the temple, I hadn't eaten yet and it was late at night. I was hungry and it completely escaped me that I had in fact had a large lunch, I had just forgotten. Well, I was thinking about what to eat. I thought I could go home and fix some pasta, but it was late, I was tired, and I didn't want something heavy before bed.

I was driving along thinking about all the food places I would pass along the way and which one might be suitable. Nothing seemed satisfactory. I had completely forgotten about Dairy Queen until I was about a block away and saw the sign.

Ice cream was perfect! Ice cream is always perfect for me, truth be told. Well, once I had that decided the rest was easy.

So, what's my point?

I have in other essays written about concentration and intention. Today I want to bring up motivation, which isn't too far off from intention and priority. If we really want something we find a way to get it done or at least to try. If we really want something we reorient our life so it becomes a priority. And all of that is easier if we really like what ever it is we are doing or trying to achieve.

So we have concentration, intention, and motivation.

When we are able to approach the Dharma with joy and delight we are able to go much further in our practice. When we have joy in our practice we are less likely to be distracted or become sidetracked. All of that enables us to have even greater joy. But when we cling too tightly to effort and form and correctness we in effect strangle out the delightfulness of Buddhism.

Practice the Dharma as if it were and ice cream cone. Enjoy it or it will melt in your hand.

> Are you able to chant until you are full, or do you watch the clock? Is your practice time oriented or fullness oriented? Is it delightful?
>
> Do you relegate your practice to only certain times, and then forget about it the rest of the time?

Beginning Again

At the beginning of the New Year we traditionally make resolutions, we decided that there are certain things we wish to accomplish and we make up our minds to do so. Here it is and we are a few days from having one fourth of the year gone by. How are you doing with your New Year resolutions? Did you make any? Are you still following them? Perhaps you changed them and are trying something else instead?

I was looking at a web site recently called "The Happiness Project." I was naturally intrigued by the title and wanted to see what the creator had to say and what the site was about.

The purpose of the site is to help those who use it to become happy, however they personally define it. There are options for not just personal happiness but group happiness as well. You might check it out if you are interested.

I notice that the first thing on the list of suggestions, though the list can be worked in any order, is 'resolution'. I think we all are pretty familiar with making a resolution. What I found interesting was the hint to make the resolution in the form of concrete actions. So instead of merely saying I want a clean house, frame the resolution something like 'I will clean my bedroom every week'. You know something you can track and measure and leads to the fulfillment of the larger goal.

We are first introduced to Buddhism, or we seek it out on our own and we decide that we too would like to become enlightened. We may approach the problem in any number of different ways.

It has been my experience that those people who make a determination to do something specific each day are the happiest. In Nichiren Shu we suggest that every day we recite a portion of the Lotus Sutra and chant Odaimoku. The idea being this gives a person some specific attainable goal. The result is that over time with the accumulation of these small daily goals a person finds that their life situation changes.

The transformation, the objective of enlightenment, is reached gradually and yet every step along the way is enlightenment.

> When you set goals do you consider rather the things required to reach that goal?
>
> For example, you might say I want a new car and I am determined to get a new car by the end of the year. That is fine, but what is missing is setting out a way to accomplish the goal. It might be more rewarding and doable if instead you said each month I am going to save X# dollars. Further it might be beneficial to say each week I am going to not buy a coffee every morning and thereby save X# dollars toward my monthly goal which will make it possible to buy the new car. See how that might work?

Freedom

Perhaps sometimes you feel as if you have no choice in daily matters. Certain chores must be accomplished, tasks fulfilled. Work needs to be completed. Money must be earned. The house needs maintenance, or at least kept clean. The list seems to go on and on, and increasingly we may feel we have no control over either the contents of the list or even who is actually making the list.

Perhaps you identify with these feelings. Perhaps sometimes you may feel helpless. And in some ways and for some things we really may have few if any choices. Except we do have one big choice in all things we do.

We have a choice over how we carry out the activities of our daily life. We can choose to be either weighted down by heavy burdens or we can choose to approach our obligations with a joyful heart.

It is a fact that our perception is a very powerful influence over our life condition. How we choose to view things affects how we experience those things. When we can look at our lives as lives that are continually manifesting the benefit of the Lotus Sutra we can experience greater joy.

Is this merely mind over matter? I would say not. The reason why I would disagree is because we are not relying on some empty promise. Because we can know the outcome we have a freedom to enjoy the process. And we truly do know the outcome if we maintain our consistent daily effort and practice of the Lotus Sutra.

If there were uncertainty about the outcome of our practice and belief in the Lotus Sutra, then we might feel there was no hope of becoming happy. Without the hope of happiness we may become discouraged and consider all of our experiences as one burden after another. We do need to live that way.

The ability to look cheerfully towards every day and everything fundamentally stems from the promise of enlightenment through your faith and practice.

> Is your life a series of chores or burdens, or is it full of rich opportunities to practice and express your Buddha potential?
>
> Pick out one thing you do that sometimes feels like a chore. Now see if there is another way of viewing the burden to turn it around to a chance to fulfill your mission as a Bodhisattva.

Comfort For Others

How we can benefit others, how we can turn the self-work we do outward. Our own enlightenment cannot occur outside the context of the people we interact with. Plus we have that first Bodhisattva vow thingy to consider, you know, helping others to attain enlightenment even before ourselves. Tricky that.

Appreciation, genuine and sincere, for other people is an important practice. Remember it isn't that someone does something for us and we thank them, although that we should definitely practice. The kind of appreciation we can try to practice is an expression of the value of their very existence, their presence in our life, good or bad. Regardless of the energy they bring us, they allow us to change to grow and to practice the Bodhisattva way.

Here's the sticky wicket, though, if there is one. We need to do so honestly and genuinely. It doesn't work quite as well and it isn't quite as connecting if it is mere formality. Here are some suggestions; give comfort without lying, smile without hesitation, give without expectation, and guide without misleading.

Now that's a lot of stuff to do. I'll probably need to remind myself about these later on. But for now it does give us some things to work on. They are not impossible, but they may be unfamiliar. That's all right; we're just trying things one step at a time, little by little.

I think, as I look at the list, perhaps the hardest thing to do is to give without expectation. For you it may be something else. But to sustain appreciation and generosity takes a great deal of effort and it is hard to do that when there is no reciprocation or recognition. Very, very, hard.

But keeping in mind that the other person may not be aware of or able to receive your efforts. Perhaps they are suffering so greatly and they are not used to someone being kind. Or maybe the only kindness they have experienced was a ploy to use them.

> Consider this list again as a starting point for connecting with others:
>
> Give comfort without lying
> Smile without hesitation
> Give without expectation
> Guide without misleading.

Connecting Through Listening

The past couple essays were about things that others appreciate us doing for them. One thing everyone appreciates is being listened to. I am sure you know there is a difference between hearing and listening. I kind of like to think of it as there is an ear in hearing there's a process in list-ening.

Sometimes we may interact with people who are not able to articulate their thoughts and feelings, I know I have had that experience. I have had the experience both as a listener and as a speaker. Sometimes we all have moments where we either do not or are not able to clearly say what we want.

I am not sure about you, however I know that when I am trying to communicate, but not having success, and the person is patient with me I don't get frustrated. When they are not patient it leads to my frustration, which seldom results in better communication. What I need at those moments is for the other person to not just hear me talking but to listen to my thoughts.

Whose fault is it, mine for an inability to say what I wish or the other for not listening? Some of both, perhaps.

But what do we do when we are the person listening or hearing? How easy is it for us to really listen with our whole heart and mind?

"Listen to me attentively, and think over my words! Now I will expound the Dharma to you." - Lotus Sutra, Chapter II

As the person listening it seems that it is our responsibility to do so effectively and carefully and with compassion; even listening with an open mind and heart. Perhaps if we give the other person a moment or some encouragement we might make a connection that otherwise we would not.

Staying present with the person who is speaking, can be hard, but if we can resist the temptation to 'leave' with our mind, we may find a way to support the person. When we listen we might discover things to engage the other person in by asking questions.

> Listen attentively, and think over the words, and then Buddha expounds the Dharma to you. You may have heard a Dharma teaching or read the Lotus Sutra for yourself, but doing so is not the same thing as having the Dharma expounded to you. Listening attentively means setting aside our personal interpretation and opening up our heart to the Dharma truth, which is transmitted from and to the heart.

Being A Guide

Continuing on with ideas on helping others, today let's look at being a guide. I kind of like the image of a guide as someone who offers assistance as another person explores, though certainly not all guides do this. Helping out other people, providing comfort, offering encouragement, listening to their stories, and if help is requested offering to guide them to their own solutions.

An effective guide does not do all the exploring or leading but is most effective when they offer opportunities for people to find their own discoveries and amazements. I know I really do not enjoy going on tours where the guide thinks they know

it all and make it clear that they are going to tell you everything you aught to know about such and such. Usually I find they have no clue as to what I am interested in and are only telling me what they are interested in. Let's not do that.

We may think we are being generous when we are providing answers to other peoples problems but if we don't allow them the freedom to actually learn it for themselves then we are in effect being stingy because in some ways our own ideas from our oh so clever minds are potentially a lesser vehicle.

My solution to your problem is not the same as your solution to your problem. Just because a person has learned the multiplication tables does not mean they can multiply.

> What are your feelings about how a guide should be?
>
> Are you able to be that kind of guide for someone?
>
> Are you able to guide yourself in such a way that sets aside accumulated knowledge and creates opportunities for new discovery?

Feelings Now

As I write this it is Sunday morning. I've been trying to make a habit of getting up early with the first thing I do is grab my caffeine and start writing. I have found that for some reason within a few minutes of arising my mind is just ripe for picking out ideas. Then after I write for an hour or so I go clean the altar and start my morning service. This also serves the purpose of emptying my mind so I can approach the Buddha and be receptive to his mind.

I don't know what your routine is and whether you have discovered your perfect spot for inspiration or contemplation. It might be good to find some time, even if only 5 or 10 minutes.

I read an article that put forth the idea that if we want to change something what we were really experiencing was a desire to feel differently. I think I concur with this thinking.

Consider the model for nonviolent communication, where changing ourselves begins as a communication that takes place with our self. Frequently though we don't know how to engage in dialogue with ourselves in order to uncover our unhappiness.

Asking our self, what am I feeling when these ideas come up? What am I feeling when I want to change? What am I feeling when I think I need a new gadget? Before we rush out to satisfy the urge if we can cultivate the instinct to inquire into the nature of the feeling, then we can progress to the next step and uncover what our real need is.

Perhaps it isn't that the grass will be greener on the other side, it is just we need to water the grass on our own side.

If we cannot identify our feelings then we may seek satisfaction in ways that do not actual eliminate the feeling but temporarily address craving.

When we work with the feeling then we can identify a need, which will satisfy that felling and not be victim to craving and grasping.

In Nonviolent communication the process is; observe the situation, identify the feeling, identify the need that will address the feeling not the situation. This is a difficult process but you can begin by doing a little every day, perhaps as you conclude your daily service. Be in touch with your needs, your being, and not so tightly wound up in your doings.

> For a listing of feeling words you might consider investigating Non Violent Communication's web page.
>
> It has been my experience as a Chaplain that people lack the vocabulary and practice of examining feelings. (Hint: "feels like" is not a feeling)

No Wasted Effort

Aren't you afraid you won't make it?

I can hardly count the number of times someone has said that to me when I have tried to do something they felt I could not do. I'll be perfectly honest, there have been times when I have let the thought seep in to my psyche. Generally though I don't entertain the notion too seriously.

It is difficult to reprogram your mind to respond to different messages from those currently playing. I won't pretend to oversimplify the process. If however a person is able to change the outlook on failure and view it as an opportunity to explore possibilities I think it leads to greater happiness.

I also firmly believe that, especially in Buddhism there is no wasted effort. Anything we do, no matter how seemingly small and insignificant, and no matter if we completely succeed or not, is not a wasted effort.

Every day we each probably spend a large amount of time and energy on many things that are not nearly as significant or meaningful or important as attaining enlightenment. We also, I suspect, spend a lot of energy worrying about what we are incapable of doing. Have you at one time or another said to yourself something to the effect of, 'I might as well not even try, I know I'll fail'?

When I was training to become a priest, I was at an advanced age. There were many potential places where I could have failed, and some folks were always eager to point out that I might not make it. In my mind and even on occasion I said, 'there is no wasted effort in Buddhism.'

If you think about this, no matter had I succeeded or not I would have learned and experienced more even in failure than I would have not trying.

As I mentioned at the beginning I know it isn't easy to change one's outlook on life. That too takes tremendous, even heroic effort. Even to just try for one moment to change our thinking for many may seem impossible or wrought with potential failure. Please do not think that because you are incapable of succeeding today, that it was without benefit. Every attempt, no matter how small, is actually a victory in itself. How heroic the attempt!

> Try saying to yourself the next time you face the possibility of failure; "There is no wasted effort in Buddhism."
>
> If we open ourselves up to opportunities to learn and live life then untold joys await us.

Remember:
"When you have great joy you will become Buddhas!"
Lotus Sutra Chapter II

Connect with me online:

Twitter: @ryusho @myoshoji

Facebook: https//www.facebook.com/Ryusho

Blog: www.myoshoji.org/blog

Made in the USA
Las Vegas, NV
26 May 2024

90376453R00085